EMP

Prepping for Tomorrow Series

A Preparedness Guide by

Bobby Akart

&

The Staff of Freedom Preppers

First edition.

Copyright Information

NOTE: Throughout this book, numerous references will be made to the EMP Commission Report issued to Congress. We suggest you review the Executive Summary prior to reading this analysis contained in EMP: Electromagnetic Pulse.

DEDICATIONS

To the love of my life, thank you for making the sacrifices
necessary so I may pursue this dream.

To the Princesses of the Palace, my little marauders in training,
you have no idea how much happiness you bring
to your Mommy and me.

To my fellow preppers;
never be ashamed of adopting a preparedness lifestyle.

ACKNOWLEDGEMENTS

Writing a book that is both informative, and entertaining requires a
tremendous team effort. Writing is the easy part. For their efforts in
making The Prepping for Tomorrow series a reality, I would like to
thank Hristo Argirov Kovatliev for his incredible cover art, Sabrina
Jean for making this important work reader-friendly, Stef Mcdaid for
making this manuscript decipherable on so many formats, and The
Team—whose advice, friendship and attention to detail is priceless.

Thank you!

ABOUT THE AUTHOR

An Amazon Top 100 Author and author of four #1 Bestsellers:

CYBER WARFARE – #1 bestseller in eight categories including Politics, Social Sciences; Business, Money; Engineering, Transportation: Science, Technology' International Politics

EMP: ELECTROMAGNETIC PULSE – #1 bestseller in four categories including International Politics, Arms Control; Physics; Politics, Social Sciences; Engineering, Transportation

SEEDS OF LIBERTY – #1 bestseller in three categories including Politics, Social Sciences; Modern History; Sociology

EVIL, MEET OPPORTUNITY – #1 bestseller in two categories including Action, Adventure; Contemporary Fiction

Bobby Akart has provided his readers a diverse range of topics that are both informative and entertaining. His attention to detail and impeccable research has allowed him to write bestselling books in several fiction and non-fiction genres.

Born and raised in Tennessee, Bobby received his bachelor's degree with a dual major in Economics and Political Science. He not only understands how the economy works, but the profound effect politics has on the economy as well. After completing his undergraduate degree at Tennessee in three years, he entered the dual-degree program, obtaining a Juris Doctor combined with an MBA—Master of Business Administration at the age of twenty-three.

His education perfectly suited him for his legal career in banking, trusts, and investment banking. As his legal career flourished, business opportunities arose, including the operation of restaurants and the development of real estate. But after meeting and marrying the love of his life, they left the corporate world and developed online businesses.

A life-changing event led them to Muddy Pond, Tennessee where he and his wife lead a self-sustainable, preparedness lifestyle. Bobby and his wife are unabashed preppers and share their expert knowledge of prepping via their website www.FreedomPreppers.com.

Bobby lives in the back woods of the Cumberland Plateau with his wife and fellow author, Danni Elle, their two English bulldogs, aka the Princesses of the Palace, a variety of farm animals, thirteen Pekin ducks, a herd of a dozen bunnies, and counting.

SIGN UP FOR EMAIL UPDATES and receive a **FREE BOOK** from one of his bestselling series. You can contact Bobby directly by email (BobbyAkart@gmail.com) or through his website

www.BobbyAkart.com

EPIGRAPH

I know not with what weapons World War III will be fought, but
World War IV will be fought with sticks and stones.
~Albert Einstein

*****

Civilization is hideously fragile.
There's not much between us & the horrors underneath, just about a
coat of varnish.
~ CP Snow

*****

The time to repair the roof is when the sun is shining.
~ John F. Kennedy

*****

By failing to prepare, you are preparing to fail.
~ Benjamin Franklin

*****

Because you never know when the day before
is the day before.
Prepare for tomorrow!

Contents

ABOUT EMP: ELECTROMAGNETIC PULSE AND THE PREPPING FOR TOMORROW SERIES

*Because you never know when the day before —
is the day before.
Prepare for tomorrow!*

Author Bobby Akart, the founder of Freedom Preppers, has been a tireless proponent of adopting a preparedness lifestyle. As he learned prepping tips and techniques, he shared them with others via his writing on the American Preppers Network website, and in his bestselling book series—*The Boston Brahmin* and *Prepping for Tomorrow*.

In The Boston Brahmin series, political suspense collides with post-apocalyptic thriller fiction. Bobby's attention to detail and real-world scenarios immerses the reader in a world of geopolitical machinations and post-apocalyptic drama. Preparedness skills and techniques are interwoven in the plot in way that the reader can be given a real-world scenario to envision.

The Prepping for Tomorrow series is the culmination of Bobby's research and real-world experiences provided in a concise guide for new and experienced preppers alike.

Steven Konkoly, author of The Perseid Collapse Series, noted that Bobby has gone far above and beyond the call of duty to support and promote fellow authors. Steve added, "from the very first time I spoke with Bobby, I was impressed with his positive attitude and willingness to share. It's the kind of selflessness that makes you wonder *what's the catch?* Well, there is no catch! Bobby is just a stand-up guy—with many talents. Author Bobby Akart possesses the analytic capability of a supercomputer coupled with the expressiveness of an exceptional writer. EMP is eye-opening."

What if the preppers are right?

The media shapes public opinion in all formats including news, cinema and television shows. It should come as no surprise that everyone doesn't necessarily form an opinion on every subject. Nor should you be shocked to hear that most opinions are uninformed. We can all give countless examples of this. Most Americans are *sheeple*, unable to think for themselves. They are content to follow, and many are too lazy to do the minimal research required to have an informed opinion. Their reliance on government or media sources for information makes them susceptible to manipulation. It's simply easier to be a *sheeple*.

As a student of the preparedness lifestyle, I cringe at the media's portrayal of preppers. Initially, the brunt of the ridicule was directed at survivalists. But with the success of National Geographic's Doomsday Preppers, the concept of being a prepper hit the mainstream. Now Preppers are the target of the media's derision. I have my opinion as to why that is the case, and it has its basis in politics. It is my opinion that the media is predominantly left-leaning and, as a result, does not embrace the self-sufficient lifestyle that is prepping. So, if you can't join them, beat them down—repeatedly. As a recent example, consider the media's dismantling of the Tea Party movement. I see similar attacks on preppers.

From the Associated Press: "*Sandy Hook Shooter Comes from Prepper Family.*"

From CBS: "*Local 'Preppers' Stock Up For Improbable US Ebola Crisis.*"

From Washington Post: "*'Preppers' Convinced Yellowstone Volcano Spells Doom.*"

But, what if the Preppers are right?

What if?

The Economy Collapses

The United States economy can collapse as a result of our own government's mismanagement of our national debt or external factors such as a global financial meltdown, an attack on the US Dollar, and other *predictable* events. Why do you think the Federal Reserve is so frightened of raising interest rates despite apparent underlying inflation data? Our economy is a house of cards. We are just a few steps away from a collapse of the dollar and hyperinflation.

History is replete with the rise and fall of empires. Are Americans so arrogant, or oblivious, to realize that we are in a stage of decline and collapse? Some of the signs of decline include a downward cultural spiral, an over-reliance on government and the inability to protect the integrity of a nation's borders. Sound familiar?

All empires collapse eventually. There have been no exceptions in the history of humanity.

None. All empires end when a more vigorous empire defeats them—or when their financing runs out.

What if?

Escalation of Global Conflict into a World War

Let's compile a list of the strongest, most dangerous *bad actors* on the world geopolitical stage:

Russia ~ China ~ North Korea ~ Iran ~ Syria ~ ISIS ~ Al Qaeda

What do these seven geopolitical foes have in common? They both hate and disrespect the United States! Think of the Seven Deadly Sins: Lust, Gluttony, Greed, Sloth, Wrath, Envy, Pride. All of these relate to the attitudes of these *bad actors* towards the United States. Is it that far-fetched that one or more of these could band together to bring the mighty United States of America to its knees? Remember the words of the great Chinese General Sun Tzu — *the enemy of my enemy is my friend*. Except ISIS and Al Qaeda, the five nations comprising this group considers each other allies.

The assassination of an Archduke precipitated World War I, but the underlying causes were geopolitical tensions in Europe. Twenty million people died during the war, followed by another seventy million post-war due to famine and the Spanish Flu. Are we naive to think that something like this couldn't happen again? *Geopolitical tensions* – sound familiar?

Tensions arising from invasions of other sovereign territories around the world were the principal cause of World War II. It escalated into a global conflict with the Japanese attack on Pearl Harbor. Today, Russia has invaded Ukraine. China prepares to exert more of its dominance in Asia. ISIS is taking over large parts of the Middle East to form an Islamic State. Some might say— *not our problem*. But what if one of the *bad actors* mentioned above decide to make it our problem with an attack on the heartland along the lines of Pearl Harbor? Is that so implausible? Remember 9/11?

What if?

America is Attacked by Terrorists

We are vulnerable to attack because of our desire to provide freedom to all Americans, but especially because of political correctness. We are not allowed to use racial profiling to identify a potential terrorist. Our southern border is a sieve. We refuse to ban flights from Ebola-stricken countries for fear of being labeled racist. Our military has been weakened by prolonged wars and budget cuts.

Our enemies can come at us in so many ways. A day does not go by without news of a cyber-terrorism incident. What if these cyber attacks are just a series of trial runs before one massive, coordinated attack on our banking, governmental and utility servers? An electromagnetic pulse delivered by a nuclear warhead or a series of electromagnetic pulse weapons fired at strategic locations across the country could bring down our power grid. For the first time, Russia has more deployed nuclear assets than the United States does. Can you say *outnumbered?*

What if?

Widespread Pandemic or BioTerror

Our government was intent on *calming the fears* of the American people as to the likelihood of the Ebola virus hitting US soil. The presence of the Ebola virus came as a result of bringing Ebola-stricken health care workers into the country. Keep in mind, that these were people who were experts in treating Ebola and who were provided all of the necessary equipment to prevent contracting Ebola. As the CDC was calming our fears, a Nigerian national flew into Dallas with Ebola, potentially infecting hundreds and ultimately dying while in the government's care.

The question has to be asked—*What is wrong with a little fear amongst the masses?*

Fear is a great motivator. It is designed to be compelling, so that we take survival action in the form of fight, flight, or freeze.

In 1763, the British fortress at Fort Pitt in Delaware was under siege. Letters were exchanged between British General Jeffrey Amherst and Colonel Henry Bouquet as to proposed defensive tactics.

General Amherst suggested: "*Could it not be contrived to send the Smallpox among those disaffected tribes of Indians?*"

Weaponized smallpox. Is it not plausible that our enemies could weaponize Ebola? In the name of Jihad, is it not possible that one would contract the Ebola virus and enter the United States with the intention of creating a pandemic? The news outlets that raise these possibilities are labeled fear mongers and racists. But have you noticed that Amazon is selling out of particulate masks and other bio-hazard supplies? Fear is a great motivator.

What if?

Near Earth Object – SuperVolcano Eruption – Natural Disaster

Any of the above naturally occurring events could wreak havoc on our power grid, our atmosphere, and our climate. These are not the catastrophic events known only in science fiction movies. There is a historical precedent for them all.

A major earthquake along the New Madrid Fault in the central United States could collapse bridges over the Mississippi River. An earthquake of this magnitude, along the New Madrid happened before in 1811 and 1812. The New Madrid Seismic Zone (NMSZ) is comprised of eight states: Alabama, Arkansas, Illinois, Indiana, Kentucky, Mississippi, Missouri, and Tennessee.

The Wabash Valley Seismic Zone (WVSZ) in southern Illinois and southeast Indiana, together with the East Tennessee Seismic Zone (ETSZ) in eastern Tennessee and northeastern Alabama, constitute a significant risk of moderate-to-severe earthquakes throughout the central region of the USA.

Studies indicate that Tennessee will incur the highest level of economic damage and societal impact. According to the Mid-America Earthquake Center, over 300,000 buildings would be moderately or more severely damaged, over 290,000 people would be displaced and well over 70,000 casualties would be expected. Total direct economic losses would surpass $56 billion. Those results focus on the immediate effects of the massive earthquake itself. As preppers, we consider the additional impact in the form of societal unrest — looting, death from sickness, and murder.

The States of Missouri, Arkansas, Kentucky, and Illinois would also incur significant losses. Studies indicate a potential direct economic loss would reach over $150 billion.

The indirect financial loss due to business interruption and loss of market share is at least as high, if not far greater than, the direct economic losses. Scientists and economists predict the total financial impact of a series of NMSZ earthquakes would be likely to constitute the highest loss due to a natural disaster in U.S. history.

The economic losses and societal impact for each state should be considered separately. Since each scenario is based on a different hazard, adding results together will not reflect an accurate scenario. It's hard to gauge the potential loss of life arising from a natural disaster of this magnitude.

After the earthquake, critical infrastructure and lifelines will be heavily damaged and will be out of service for a considerable period. The resulting collapse of the power grid and transportation routes are likely to affect a region much larger than the eight states referenced above. Many hospitals nearest to the epicenter will not be able to care for its patients. Many of those injured during the disaster will have to be transported outside of the region for medical attention. Moreover, pre-disaster patients will be required to continue their care outside of the area, at fully functioning hospitals.

It is doubtful that the transportation system will be intact. Damage to the transportation system will hinder mass evacuation efforts. First responders will be severely impaired due to police and fire stations throughout the impacted region. Public shelters will be damaged and unusable after the earthquake.

The scenario described for a New Madrid Zone earthquake can be applied to other catastrophic disaster events. Strikes by bjects, NEOs, such as asteroids, can be extinction-level events. Likewise, a massive eruption of the Yellowstone SuperVolcano could result in climate change that would alter the entire food production system of the Northern Hemisphere.

What if?

The Deadly Threat of a Coronal Mass Ejection – Solar Flare

A powerful electromagnetic pulse, whether resulting from a nuclear-delivered EMP or a massive solar storm, could collapse the power grid and the critical infrastructure of our nation.

What are solar storms?

Every minute, enormous eruptions of magnetically-charged plasma are emitted from the sun's roiling interior, exploding outward into space. Known as coronal mass ejections, or CME, these moderate solar storms occur fairly regularly and harmlessly, sometimes causing spectacular auroras that illuminate the sky over the North and South poles. But even typically benign solar storms generate energy many times more powerful than our planet's combined nuclear arsenals.

Is the threat real? Renowned American astronomer, Phil Plait, who is a self-proclaimed skeptic, is known as The Bad Astronomer because of his work in debunking common misunderstandings about space events. "People sometimes ask me if anything in astronomy worries me," says Plait, when asked about the threat of a deadly CME. "Something like this is near the top of the list."

There is good reason to be concerned. A National Academy of Sciences study found there is a twelve percent chance that a monster solar storm will strike Earth within the next decade. A solar event of that magnitude could cause two trillion dollars' worth of damage in the first year of recovery alone—twenty-times the cost of Hurricane Katrina.

But, what about the human cost? Studies frequently cite economic loss. How would the destruction of the power grid and other critical infrastructure; like the internet, banking, and government be affected? Has such a storm ever hit Earth?

Yes, several times. Imagine our way of life without power for weeks on end, as a result of a massive solar flare striking the Earth. It happened in 1859, in what is commonly referred to as the Carrington Event.

On Sept. 1, 1859, British astronomer Richard Carrington noticed a brilliant solar flare over England. In the days that followed, a succession of coronal mass ejections struck Earth head-on. Auroras illuminated the night sky from Africa to Hawaii. "The light appeared to cover the whole firmament," one Baltimore newspaper reported. "It had an indescribable softness and delicacy." The effects were more than aesthetic. EMPs from the storm caused telegraph systems — known as the *Victorian internet* — to fail throughout North America and Europe; in some cases, lines sparked and offices caught fire. Otherwise, the damage was minimal.

Nonetheless, for telegraph operators in the Americas and Europe, the experience caused chaos. Many found that their lines were just unusable—they could neither send nor receive messages. Others were able to operate even with their power supplies turned off, using only the current in the air from the solar storm.

From historical reports, one telegraph operator said, "The line was in perfect order, and skilled operators worked incessantly from eight o'clock last evening until one o'clock this morning to transmit, in an intelligible form, four hundred words of the report per steamer Indian for the Associated Press."

Other operators experienced physical danger. Washington, D.C. operator, Frank Royce said, "I received a very severe electric shock, which stunned me for an instant. An old man who was sitting facing me, and but a few feet distant, said that he saw a spark of fire jump from my forehead to the sounder."

At the time, the telegraph was a new technology and never experienced technical difficulties of this type. But the story offers an important warning for modern society. The Carrington Event provides evidence of the fragility of electrical infrastructure. Scientific

American reported in October of 1859: "The electromagnetic basis of the various phenomena was identified relatively quickly. A connection between the northern lights and forces of electricity and magnetism is now fully established."

This event was long before humanity became utterly reliant on electronics — as it was when history repeated itself 153 years later.

In 1989, a far smaller solar flare sent a pulse of radiation that left six million people in Quebec without power for up to nine hours. Much more alarming, was a solar super storm that barely missed Earth in July 2012. Astronomers say the sun spewed out a huge magnetic cloud that tracked straight through our planet's orbit. Fortunately, for civilization, the Earth was elsewhere in its path around the sun at the time but had the storm roared through nine days earlier, a worst-case scenario would have occurred. Satellites involved in crucial global communications (including GPS) would have been ruined, large electrical transformers would have been destroyed, and ATMs would have stopped functioning. The internet would have been disabled on a massive scale. Most people wouldn't have been able to flush toilets, which rely on electric pumps.

Three years later, "we would still be picking up the pieces," says astronomer Daniel Baker. "The July 2012 storm was, in all respects, at least as strong as the Carrington Event. The only difference is, *it missed*."

In a word—TEOTWAWKI
—The End Of The World As We Know It.

Over the last one hundred and fifty years, the world's critical infrastructure has become a more integral part of daily life. In the nineteenth century, telegraphs composed a comparatively small and relatively non-essential part of everyday life. Their successors today— including the electrical grid and much of the telecommunications network—are essential to modern life.

Is the current system any more protected from catastrophic interference than the telegraph of the nineteenth century? Can the power grid handle a terrorist attack, or severe weather events, or a solar storm?

There has never been a real test to prove it, but there is a robust debate about the vulnerability of the power grid. The most dangerous and costly possibilities for major catastrophes, the collapse of the nation's critical infrastructure, might visit the United States from any number of methods.

One scenario is a repeat of the solar storm as big as the 1859 Carrington Event. A solar event of this magnitude hasn't struck the earth since, although there have been smaller ones. As a result of the Quebec blackout in 1989, there were complications across the interconnected grid and a large transformer in New Jersey permanently failed.

In 2003, residents of the northeastern United States experienced a grid-down scenario. It doesn't take an unprecedented solar flare to knock out power. The combination of a few trees touching power lines, and a few power companies asleep at the wheel, plunged a section of the nation into darkness. The darkness can spread. As the difficulties at Ohio-based FirstEnergy grew and eventually cascaded over the grid, electrical service from Detroit to New York City was lost. The 2003 event was a comparatively minor episode, compared to what might have happened. Most customers had their power back within a couple of days and the transformers were relatively unaffected.

Compare that event with the incident in Auckland, New Zealand. Cables supplying power to the downtown business district failed in 1998. The center of the city went dark. Companies were forced to shutter or relocate their operations outside of the affected area. The local Auckland utility had to adopt drastic measures to move in temporary generators. They even enlisted the assistance of the world's largest cargo plane—owned by rock band *U2*, to transport massive generators into the area. It took five weeks for the power grid to be fully restored.

There are contrarians. Jeff Dagle, an electrical engineer at the Pacific Northwest National Laboratory, who served on the Northeast

Blackout Investigation Task Force argued, "one lesson of the 2003 blackout is that the power grid is more resilient than you might think."

The task force investigators pinpointed four separate root causes for the collapse, and human error played a significant role. "It took an hour for it to collapse with no one managing it," Dagle said. "They would have been just as effective if they had just gone home for the day. That to me just underscores how remarkably stable things are."

As awareness was raised by Congress, the National Academies of Science produced a report detailing the risk of a significant solar event. The 2008 NAS report paints a dire picture, based on a study conducted for FEMA and Electromagnetic Pulse Commission created by Congress.

While severe solar storms do not occur that often, they have the potential for long-term catastrophic impacts to the nation's power grid. Impacts would be felt on interdependent infrastructures. For example, the potable water distribution will be affected immediately. Pumps and purification facilities rely on electricity. The nation's food supply will be disrupted, and most perishable foods will spoil and be lost within twenty-four hours. There will be immediate or eventual loss of heating/air conditioning, sewage disposal, phone service, transportation, fuel resupply, and many of the necessities that we take for granted.

According to the EMP Commission, the effects would be felt for years, and its economic costs could add up to trillions of dollars—dwarfing the cost of Hurricane Katrina. More importantly, the commission's findings stated a potential loss of life that was staggering. Within one year, according to their conclusions, ninety percent of Americans would die.

But some skeptics say it's the opposite. Jon Wellinghoff, who served as Chairman of the Federal Energy Regulatory Commission—commonly known as FERC, from 2009 to 2013, has sounded the alarm about the danger of an attack on the system. The heightened awareness came as a result of an April 2013 incident in Silicon Valley, California, in which a group of attackers conducted a coordinated assault on an electrical substation, knocking out twenty-seven transformers. FERC points to the fact that the U.S. power grid is broken into three big sections known as *interconnections*. There is one each for the Eastern United States, the Western United States, and— out on its own—Texas. In fact, the East and West interconnections also include much of Canada and parts of Mexico.

In a 2013 report, FERC concluded that if a limited number of substations in each of those interconnections were disabled, utilities would not be able to bring the interconnections back up again for an indeterminate amount of time. FERC's conclusion isn't classified information. This information has been in government reports and widely disseminated on the internet for years.

FERC also noted that it could take far longer to return the electrical grid to full functionality than it did in 2003. Wellinghoff said, "If you destroy the transformers—all it takes is one high-caliber bullet through a transformer case, and it's gone, you have to replace it. If there aren't spares on hand—and in the event of a coordinated attack on multiple substations, any inventory could be exhausted—it takes months to build new ones."

"Once your electricity is out, your gasoline is out, because you can't pump the gas anymore. All your transportations out, all of your financial transactions are out, of course because there are no electronics," Wellinghoff also stated.

FERC's proposed solution was to break the system into a series of *microgrids*. In the event of a cascading failure, smaller portions of the country could isolate themselves from the collapse of the grid. There is a precedent for this. Princeton University has an independent power grid. When a large part of the critical infrastructure collapsed during Superstorm Sandy, the Princeton campus became a place of refuge for residents and a command center for first responders.

These doomsday scenarios may be beside the point because the electrical grid is already subject to a series of dangerous stresses from natural disasters. Sandy showed that the assumptions used to build many parts of the electrical infrastructure were wrong. The storm surge overwhelmed the substations, causing them to flood, and subsequently fail. Experts determined that significant portions of the grid might need to be moved to higher ground.

Even away from the coasts, extreme weather can threaten the system in unexpected ways. Some systems use gas insulation, but if the temperature drops low enough, the gas composition changes and the insulation fails. Power plants in warmer places like Texas aren't well-prepared for extreme cold, meaning power-generating plants could fail when the population needs them the most to provide power for heat. As utilities rely more heavily on natural gas to generate power, there's a danger of demand exceeding supply. A likely scenario is a blizzard, in which everyone cranks up their propane or natural gas-powered heating systems. As the system becomes overwhelmed, the gas company can't provide to everyone. Power providers don't necessarily have the first right of refusal from their sources, so they could lose their supply and be forced to power down in the middle of a winter storm.

Summer doesn't necessarily offer any respite. Even prolonged droughts can play a role. As consumers turn up their air conditioners, requests for more power will increase. There can be a ratcheting effect. If there are several days of consistently high temperatures, buildings will never cool completely. The demand from local utilities will peak higher and higher each day. Power plants rely upon groundwater to cool their systems. They will struggle to maintain cooling as the water itself heats up. Droughts can diminish the power from hydroelectric plants, especially in the western United States.

If such extreme weather continues to be the norm, the chaos that was unleashed on the grid by Sandy may have been a preview of the kinds of disruptions to the grid, that might become commonplace. As the New York Herald argued in 1859, referring to the Carrington event, "Phenomena are not supposed to have any reference to things past—only to things to come. Therefore, the aurora borealis must be connected with something in the future—war, or pestilence, or famine." Although the impact of solar storms was not fully understood at the time, the prediction of catastrophe remains valid.

What protective measures are possible?

The Obama administration has taken steps to replace some of the aging satellites that monitor space weather, and extra-high-voltage transformers that are vulnerable to solar storms. The administration's new plan also calls for scientists to establish benchmarks for weather events in space, incorporating something similar to the Richter scale. The strategy also includes assessing the vulnerability of the power grid, increasing international cooperation, and improving solar-flare forecast technology — a crucial step.

But Dr. Peter Pry, Chairman of the EMP Commission, says that neither the White House, nor Congress, is taking the threat seriously enough or acting with the appropriate urgency. According to Dr. Pry, it would cost about two billion dollars— the amount of foreign aid we give to Pakistan — to harden the nation's power grid to minimize the damage from either a nuclear EMP or a solar flare. "If we suspended that [aid] for one year and put it toward hardening the electrical grid," Pry says, "we could protect the American people from this threat."

Is this Science Fiction or Reality?

All of the events described above are plausible and have their roots in history. What could happen? Global Panic. Martial Law. Travel Restrictions. Food and Water Shortages. An Overload of the Medical System. Societal Collapse. Economic Collapse.

This is why we prep. Prepping is insurance against both natural and man-made catastrophic events. The government now requires you to carry medical insurance. Your homeowner's insurance may include damage from tornadoes. Even though you may never incur damage from a tornado, you pay for that coverage monthly nonetheless. This is what preppers do. We allocate time and resources to protect our families, in the event of seemingly unlikely events, but events that are occurring daily or have historical precedent.

At Freedom Preppers, we hope none of these catastrophic events occur, but *what if?*

Cyber Warfare

We explored this concept in depth with the first book released into the *Prepping for Tomorrow* series, entitled *Cyber Warfare*. A #1 bestseller in an unprecedented eight Amazon categories, *Cyber Warfare* is a primer on the threats that we face as a nation, from the bad actors mentioned earlier. It explores the history of cyber attacks and discusses the nuances of the terminology. The United States and its allies have evolved over the past decade in their policies. Throughout the book, the problem of attribution is explored as cyber space allows hackers a convenient place to hide.

The all-important issue is raised: *When does a cyber attack become an act of war?*

After a thorough review of the threat that a devastating cyber attack poses for America, in particular, the critical infrastructure, Cyber Warfare provides preparedness solutions. Like Cyber Warfare, this guide will also help you answer the question:

What if the preppers are right?

Simply put, a cyber attack is a deliberate exploitation of computer systems. Cyber attacks are used to gain access to information, but can also be used to alter computer code, insert malware, or take over the operations of a computer-driven network.

Why would terrorists bother with an elaborate and dangerous physical operation—complete with all the recon and planning of a black ops mission—when they could achieve the same effect from the comfort of their home? An effective cyber attack could, if cleverly designed, produce a great deal of physical damage very quickly. The sheer amount of interconnections in digital operations would mean that such an attack could bypass fail-safes in the physical infrastructure that would normally stop cascading failures.

A single string of ones and zeros could have a significant impact. If a computer hacker could command all the circuit breakers in a utility to open, the system would be overloaded. Power utility personnel sitting in the control room could do that, but a proficient cyber-terrorist could do it as well. In fact, smart-grid technologies are more susceptible to common computer failures. New features that have been added to make the system easily manageable, might render it more vulnerable.

At least one major public official downplays the cyber attack scenario. The nation's top disaster responder, FEMA director, Craig Fugate shrugs at the threat of a power grid collapse.

"When have people panicked? Generally what you find is the birth rate goes up nine months later," he said, then turned more serious: "People are much more resilient than the professionals would give them credit for. Would it be unpleasant? Yes. Would it be uncomfortable? Have you ever seen the power go out, and traffic signals stop working? Traffic's hell, but people figure it out."

Fugate's big worry in a mass outage is communication, he has said. When people can get information and know how long power will be out, they will handle it much better.

Don't worry, the government will take care of you. Naïve.

Is there a precedent for the use of a cyber attack to take down a nation's power grid? Let's look at 2015.

On March 31, 2015, the majority of homes and businesses in Turkey lost power as the result of alleged cyber attack by Iranian proxies. Analysts initially declared this the first full-blown blackout utilizing Cyber Warfare. Months later, Turkey announced the blackout was caused by an equipment malfunction, not by a cyber attack. One has to wonder if the Turkish government denied the cyber intrusion in order to avoid admission of the vulnerability of its critical infrastructure to cyber attack.

On December 23, 2015, when a cyber attack on the power grid in Ukraine thrust that part of the nation into darkness, nearly 80,000 homes in Ukraine's Ivano-Frankivsk region were without power. Believed to be part of Ukraine-Russian hostilities in the region, initial reports pointed to Russian hackers armed with a malware called *BlackEnergy*. This is the most recent successful attack on a power grid by hackers with the largest impact on a nation.

Reports reveal that a Russian proxy group known as *Sandworm* carried out the attack by remotely switching breakers to cut power, following the installation of the *BlackEnergy* malware in order to prevent technicians from identifying the attack. The attack also included a denial of service to the utility's phone systems. Robert Lee, a former US Air Force cyber warfare operations officer who helped compile the report, was quoted by Reuters as saying, "This was a multi-pronged attack against multiple facilities. It was highly coordinated with very professional logistics. They sort of blinded them in every way possible."

In poll after poll, one of the threats that concerns preppers is the use of a cyber attack to cause a grid-down scenario. There are many bad actors on the international stage. Each one is capable of wreaking havoc in the US, by shutting down our power grid and enjoying the resulting chaos.

No bombs. No bullets. No swordfights. Just a few keystrokes on the computer, and we're done.

What if?

EMP: Electromagnetic Pulse

EMP: Electromagnetic Pulse is a primer on the threats we face as a nation from an attack delivered by an Electromagnetic Pulse weapon. The constant barrage of cyber intrusions into the public and private sector have captured the news headlines in recent years, but it is time to refocus on the threat an EMP poses for our nation's critical infrastructure.

Senator Ron Johnson, of Wisconsin, Chairman of the Senate Committee on Homeland Security and Governmental Affairs, began hearings in the summer of 2015 on the threat of an EMP detonation over the United States.

The witnesses included, among others; James Woolsey, former Director of Central Intelligence, Joseph McClelland, Director of the Office of Energy Infrastructure Security at FERC, and Christopher Currie, Director of Homeland Security and Justice with the Government Accountability Office.

Their conclusion: The threat is real, and the need for the U.S. to prepare for this eventuality is critical. Chairman Johnson, in his opening remarks, stated that although the issue of EMP has been on the government radar for years, it has largely gone ignored. He pointed out the fact that not one of the suggestions put forward by the congressionally mandated EMP Commission, formed in 2002, has been put in place.

The science behind an electromagnetic pulse might be considered complicated and frightening to some. An EMP event can occur either naturally, (through solar flares, as discussed above) or artificially, as the result of a high-altitude nuclear explosion. The high-energy particles from such an explosion would cascade down to Earth, interacting with the planet's magnetic field and destroying the electronic systems below. The resulting pulse of energy could destroy millions of transformers in America's power grid, as the pulse travelled along transformer lines.

The possibility of man-made EMP events has grown in relation to the technological sophistication of America's adversaries. It is a widely known fact, that both Russia and China already have this capability, and both countries have carried out serious work relating to the generation of EMP in recent years, as part of their respective military modernization programs.

Now, America's enemies like Iran and North Korea may not be that far behind. Iran, for example, is known to have simulated a nuclear EMP attack several years ago, using short-range missiles launched from a freighter. In 2015, the Iranians fired a medium-range missile capable of carrying a nuclear warhead. North Korea, meanwhile, has acquired the blueprints to build an EMP warhead. In July of 2013, a North Korean freighter made it all the way to the Gulf of Mexico, through the Panama Canal, carrying two nuclear-capable missiles in the ship's hold.

All of these countries have successfully orbited a number of satellites that could potentially evade U.S. early warning radars. The Strategic Defense Initiative, or Star Wars, as former President Ronald Reagan once called it, was widely panned as bizarre by political opponents and the mainstream media. Today, satellites carrying nuclear warheads are at the ideal altitude to generate an EMP across the entire continental US. Perhaps, President Reagan was right.

Scientists concur that such an attack, if it occurred, would have devastating consequences. A nuclear warhead detonated three hundred miles above St. Louis, Missouri, could collapse the entire nation's power grid. According to the EMP Commission, the recovery time from such a nationwide EMP event might be anywhere from one to ten years. In the meantime, ninety percent of Americans would likely die from starvation, disease, or societal collapse.

Are the threats of an EMP attack and Cyber Warfare mutually exclusive? Not necessarily. North Korea's recent nuclear test and dictator Kim Jong Un's claim that he has a hydrogen bomb, has shifted focus away from the cyber threat and onto EMP once again. Although the focus of attention has shifted, at least temporarily, away from cyber threats, the North Korean nuclear threat is just another dimension of the threat from cyber warfare.

Russia, China, Iran, and North Korea have all adopted an asymmetric warfare capability. Cyber warfare is not limited to computer viruses and hacking but is a combined-arms operation that includes the coordinated use of physical sabotage and an EMP attack. Our enemies consider a high-altitude nuclear EMP attack as the ultimate weapon. North Korea's recent low-yield nuclear test, and its claim that it has a hydrogen bomb, are confirmation of the Congressional EMP Commission's findings that North Korea is attempting to acquire a super-EMP weapon —a low-yield hydrogen bomb.

There are solutions, and the clarion bell has been rung. Our nation's leaders have a duty to protect the homeland. This book is intended to raise awareness of the threat, and provide the reader with preparedness solutions. ***EMP: Electromagnetic Pulse*** will also help you answer the question:

What if?

**EMP: A threat from above to America's soft underbelly below.
The clock is ticking. One second after. One year after.**

PART ONE

WHAT IS AN ELECTROMAGNETIC PULSE?

CHAPTER ONE
LET'S GET TECHNICAL

Author's Note: Bear with us here. Understanding the technical aspect of electromagnetic pulse technology is critical to assessing the threat and making your preparations.

An electromagnetic pulse—EMP, is an intense burst of electromagnetic energy caused by an abrupt, rapid acceleration of charged particles, usually electrons. An EMP can contain elements of energy over a large part of the electromagnetic spectrum, from very-low-frequency radio, to ultraviolet, wavelengths.

A typical example is a lightning strike that produces a localized EMP. As the lightning makes contact, it can direct a large electrical current in nearby wires. A single current surge can damage sensitive electronic circuitry, such as wires and connection contained in computers and ancillary equipment. Most of us are aware that electronic and communications systems should have some form of protection against the effects of the surge of electricity caused by a lightning strike. Surge protection devices, AC outlets, and modem jacks offer limited protection against the naturally-occurring electromagnetic pulse caused by lightning.

By definition, an *explosion* results from the very rapid release of a large amount of energy within a limited space. This definition applies to a lightning strike, a conventional explosive like dynamite, as well as for a nuclear detonation. However, the energy produced by any one of these *explosions* results from different means.

The sudden release of energy causes a considerable increase of temperature and pressure so that all the materials present are converted into hot, compressed gasses. These gasses reach an extremely high temperature and an increase in pressure, as they expand rapidly. This expansion initiates a pressure wave, or shock wave in its surroundings, whether ground, air, or water. One of the common characteristics of any explosion is a sudden increase of pressure at the front of the resulting wave, followed by a gradual decrease behind it. A shock wave of any magnitude is commonly referred to as a *blast wave* because it resembles, and is often accompanied by, a very strong wind.

Understand that all explosions are relative. The effects of the shock wave are directly proportional to the amount of electromagnetic energy associated with the detonation. Its force and effect depend on the quantity of energy associated with the explosion.

Like most conventional munitions, nuclear weapons impact its target with a blast wave. There are significant differences, however. Nuclear explosions are millions of times more powerful than the largest of conventional weapon detonations. For the release of the tremendous amount of energy associated with a nuclear weapon, the mass of the nuclear explosive must be much less than that of a conventional high explosive. Also, the temperatures reached in a nuclear explosion are much higher.

One of the principal differences between conventional weapons and a nuclear EMP is the powerful electrical currents created by the blast. For that reason, the effectiveness of the conventional bomb and a nuclear EMP differ because the target is vastly different. Conventional weapons seek out hard targets—a surface burst. Nuclear EMPs seek out a high-altitude location above the Earth's surface—an air burst.

CHAPTER TWO

WHAT ARE THE CHARACTERISTICS OF A NUCLEAR EMP?

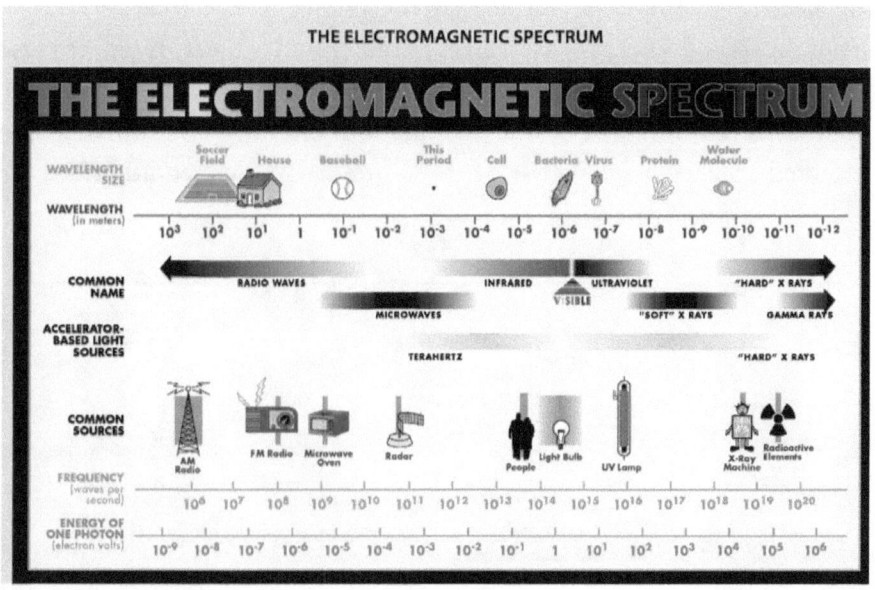

THE ELECTROMAGNETIC SPECTRUM

A nuclear EMP has three components—E1, E2, and E3, as defined by the International Electrotechnical Commission, or IEC.

The E3 pulse is a very slow pulse that can last anywhere from ten seconds to several minutes. An E3 is common in geomagnetic disturbances from the sun—*solar storms*, and will vary in effect, based upon the strength of a solar induced EMP.

The E2 pulse usually lasting less than a second, is similar in strength and timing to the electrical pulses produced by lightning.

The E1 pulse is a very fast pulse that generates high voltages in electrical conductors. It is produced when gamma radiation from a powerful nuclear detonation strips away electrons from the Earth's atmosphere. The process of stripping away the electrons is

25

commonly known as the Compton Effect—the result of a high-energy photon colliding with a target, which releases the electrons. Once released, these electrons travel downward through the Earth's atmosphere at nearly the speed of light.

If the Earth did not have a magnetic field, a large vertical pulse of electric current like this would strike the area immediately below the detonation. But in reality, the Earth's magnetic field deflects the flow of electrons across the surface of the planet to create a very large, brief burst of energy—an EMP. This is why there is an inverse relationship between the height of the detonation and the surface area affected; the lower the detonation altitude—the smaller the affected area. A height burst of three hundred miles would affect the U.S. from coast-to-coast.

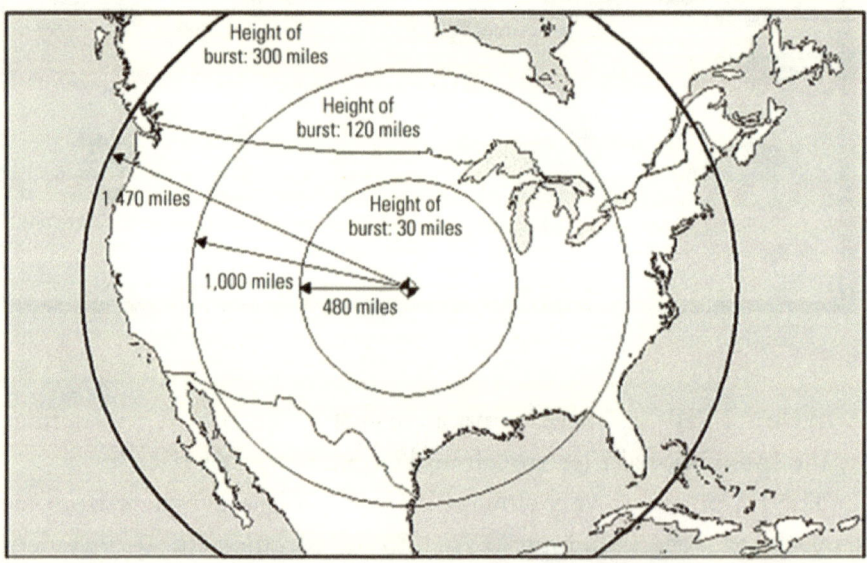

The E1 pulse causes most of its damage by overwhelming electrical breakdown voltages. An E1 pulse can destroy all forms of electronics because the surge of energy is simply too fast for ordinary surge protectors to provide sufficient protection from the enormous voltage spike.

CHAPTER THREE

WHAT ARE THE DIFFERENCES BETWEEN A NUCLEAR EMP, A CME, AND AN RF WEAPON?

As was mentioned above, an electromagnetic pulse comes in many forms, including lightning, geomagnetic disturbances from the Sun, and nuclear weapons EMP weapons.

Here, we will also introduce some of the newest technology in the form of **Radio Frequency Weapons—RFW**.

RF Weapons, also known as directed-energy weapons, use electromagnetic energy on specific frequencies to disable electronic systems. The principle is similar to that of high-power microwave (HPM) weapons. HPM systems tend to be much more sophisticated and are more likely to be in the control of technologically advanced nations. RF weapons, by contrast, are simple and low-voltage enough that they could be deployed by smaller, less technologically enhanced forces, including terrorists. In fact, they can be manufactured using parts purchased online, or at your local Radio Shack store. Instructions for assembling the components and how to use the RFW are available online as well.

In the electromagnetic spectrum, the range of frequencies for waves is from approximately 102 Hz to more than 1025 Hz. From the lowest frequencies to about 1010 Hertz is the range of long-wave radio, short-wave radio, and microwaves. These lower frequencies carry broadcast radio, television, mobile phone communications, radar, and even highly specific forms of transmission; such as those of baby monitors or garage-door openers.

Due to regulations by the Federal Communications Commission (FCC), AM—*amplitude modulation* broadcasts, take place across a frequency range from 535 kHz to 1.7MHz. The FCC has assigned the range of 5.9 to 26.1 MHz to shortwave radio, and 26.96 to 27.41 MHz to citizens' band (CB) radio. Above these levels are microwave regions assigned to very high frequency (VHF) television stations 2 through 6, then FM—*frequency modulation* radio, which occupies the range from 88 to 108 MHz. Higher still are VHF—*very high-frequency* channels 7 to 13, and UHF—*ultra high-frequency* television broadcasts. At the highest microwave ranges—around 1010 Hz—is where you will find transmissions from spacecraft.

FCC regulation is necessary to maintain security, privacy, and safety on the airwaves. If a broadcaster or receiver strays outside of its assigned range, it can intercept private communications, or potentially disrupt highly sensitive transmissions. Among the most vulnerable from a safety perspective, are the communications between an aircraft cockpit and the control tower, which could result in grave consequences if disrupted, even for a few seconds.

Why is this important? High-power microwave weaponry produces a voltage and intensity capable of shutting off the computer systems of an aircraft long enough that a pilot would be unable to operate his navigational controls, potentially causing a crash. With an RF weapon, the intensity of the signal is smaller, but if properly directed, it could possibly disrupt aircraft communication systems long enough to bring down the plane. It could cause the computers to reset, or disrupt safety sensors, navigation systems, data recorders, or control systems. Enough errors in these sensitive flight components, particularly in the highly computerized aircraft of today, might be sufficient to force a plane out of the sky. This threat will be discussed in more depth, as it relates to RFW use by terrorists, namely ISIS.

Concerns over RF interference initially resulted in the prohibition against cell phone, radio, or computer operation aboard an aircraft, from the time of preparation for takeoff, until after it lands. Such relatively weak and harmless electronic devices could interfere with vital flight communications. Imagine the harm that could be done by terrorists operating a directed and more powerful system with malicious intent.

Adding to the dangers of RF weaponry is its portability, allowing it to be operated from the ground. A terrorist could attack a target and seek cover in the process, rendering the sacrifice of the terrorist's life unnecessary. Furthermore, RF weaponry, as a means of electromagnetic warfare, is *clean* and virtually untraceable.

To summarize, RF Weapons operate as a high-frequency pulse, in the E1 range, similar to a nuclear EMP. The primary differences are that the RF Weapon is localized—directed at a particular target— while a high-altitude EMP is intended to have a broad impact, depending on its height of detonation.

On the other hand, a powerful **Coronal Mass Ejection, or CME,** is considered a low-frequency event—the equivalent of the E3 component of a nuclear EMP.

A CME originates in active regions on the Sun's surface from groupings of sunspots associated with frequent solar flares. When a CME is emitted from the sun, enormous quantities of electromagnetic radiation are discharged through space. When the ejection is directed towards Earth, the shock wave of the traveling mass of solar energized particles causes a disruption in the Earth's magnetosphere. This disruption is very similar to the detonation of a high-altitude nuclear EMP. These solar energized particles cause a geomagnetic storm within the Earth's upper atmosphere, creating a beautiful aurora around the North and South poles. Known as the Northern Lights, or *aurora borealis*, in the northern hemisphere, and the Southern Lights, or *aurora australis* in the southern hemisphere, these geomagnetic storms can produce beautiful skies for observers as far south as the U.S. – Canadian border.

However, depending upon the intensity of the geomagnetic storm, damage to electronics can occur. Despite this fact, there has never been a solar storm recorded that released the energy equivalent to a nuclear EMP. An additional difference, is the requirement of an antenna for the CME to directly impact electronics. Once the charged particles of a CME enter the Earth's atmosphere, they interact with power lines, electrical cords, USB cables, etc. to travel through electronics. A nuclear EMP does not require an antenna to impact electronic circuitry.

A CME is a random, relatively unpredictable event. Today's advanced technology enables scientists to detect an incoming CME twelve to seventy-two hours in advance of an impact with Earth. However, magnetic field strength and orientation of incoming plasma – key ingredients in forecasting the effect of the impact on Earth, can only be accurately measured with a lead time of fifteen to thirty minutes.

PART TWO

HISTORY OF THE
ELECTROMAGNETIC PULSE

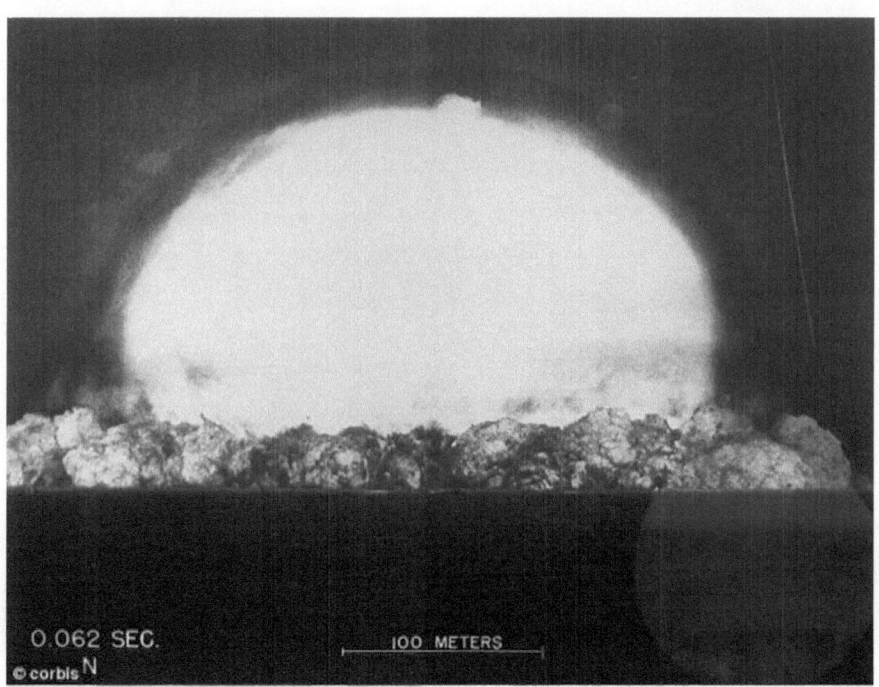

0.062 SEC.   100 METERS
© corbis

CHAPTER FOUR
SIGNIFICANT EVENTS IN THE HISTORY OF EMP

1945: Project Y, Los Alamos, New Mexico

The fact that an electromagnetic pulse is produced by a nuclear explosion was known in the earliest days of nuclear weapons testing. At 5:30 a.m. on July 16, 1945, Los Alamos scientists detonated a plutonium bomb at a test site located on the U.S. Air Force base at Alamogordo, New Mexico, approximately 120 miles south of Albuquerque. Project Y was led by famed physicist, Robert Oppenheimer. He chose the name *Trinity* for the test site, inspired by the poetry of John Donne.

When the first atomic bomb finally detonated atop a steel tower, an intense light flash and a sudden wave of heat were followed by a great burst of sound that echoed across the valley. A ball of fire rose into the sky and then was surrounded by a giant mushroom-shaped cloud that stretched approximately thirty-eight thousand feet wide. With the power equivalent to around twenty-one thousand tons of TNT, the bomb completely obliterated the steel tower on which it rested. The nuclear age had begun.

Before the Trinity test, Enrico Fermi, known as the *architect of the nuclear age*, was persuaded by Dr. Oppenheimer to join Project Y at Los Alamos, New Mexico. Part of his responsibilities were to calculate the possible electromagnetic fields produced by the explosion. His calculations led to further testing in the next decade.

1950s: Operation Buffalo, British Testing in Australia

The first in a series of atomic explosions took place at Maralinga, South Australia by a team of British scientists. *Operation Buffalo* commenced on September 27, 1956. Operation Buffalo consisted of the testing of four nuclear devices, codenamed *One Tree, Marcoo, Kite,* and *Breakaway*, respectively. *One Tree* (12.9 kilotons of TNT) and

Breakaway (10.8 kilotons of TNT) were exploded from steel towers. *Marcoo* (1.4 kilotons of TNT) was exploded at ground level. The last test, *Kite* (2.9 kilotons of TNT), was released by a Royal Air Force Vickers Valiant bomber from a height of thirty-five thousand feet. The *Kite* test was the first reported launching of a nuclear weapon from a British aircraft.

The Operation Buffalo atomic tests were the fourth in a series conducted in Australia. Throughout the 1950s, the British had fired atomic bombs on the deserted Monte Bello Islands, off the coast of Western Australia.

Before Operation Buffalo, instrumentation failures were observed during nuclear weapons testing between 1951 and 1953. Early testing by the UK, revealed a *click* heard on radio receivers when an atomic bomb was detonated. This *click* was often followed by a failure in the equipment. Later, in declassified military literature, the electronic breakdowns were attributed to radiated *radioflash*. *Radioflash* became the term used in early reports on the phenomena, now more widely known as a nuclear electromagnetic pulse. It was later discovered that the phenomena was only one part of the more wide-ranging set of effects resulting from EMPs, after the detonation of nuclear weapons.

1958: Operation Hardtack, Pacific Proving Grounds, United States

Operation Hardtack was a series of thirty-five nuclear tests conducted by the United States in 1958 at the Pacific Proving Grounds, located in the Marshall Islands. Under growing political pressure from the international community to limit nuclear testing, the United States conducted a series of high altitude, multi-megaton tests, to study their usefulness for anti-ballistic missile warheads. In the process, the high-altitude electromagnetic pulse was discovered. After the U.S. had completed six of the high-altitude nuclear tests, the unexpected results that were associated with the EMP effect raised many new questions. The U.S. Government Project Officer's Interim Report on the Starfish Prime project read, in part:

"Previous high-altitude nuclear tests: YUCCA, TEAK, and

ORANGE, plus the three ARGUS shots were poorly instrumented and hastily executed. Despite thorough studies of the meager data, present models of these bursts are sketchy and tentative. These models are too uncertain to permit extrapolation to other altitudes and yields with any confidence. Thus, there is a strong need, not only for better instrumentation but for further tests covering a range of altitudes and yields."

The EMP effect observations generated considerable interest within the nuclear science community, leading to additional testing into the 1960's.

Following the testing by the British and the U.S. in the latter part of the 1950's, the Soviet Union called for a ban on atmospheric testing of nuclear weapons and unilaterally halted its nuclear program. The U.S. paused testing for a short time. In late 1961, Nikita Khrushchev, Secretary of the Communist Party of the Soviet Union, was forced to break the moratorium, under internal political pressures. The Soviets began testing once again. The nuclear arms race was on.

1962: Starfish Prime, Operation Fishbowl, United States

Intelligence received from the 1961 Soviet tests raised alarms within U.S. military agencies. Following an analysis of the results, the U.S. became concerned that a Soviet nuclear bomb detonated in space could possibly damage or destroy our advanced weaponry. Consequently, American scientists ratcheted up their nuclear testing program. Although there was some data from the previous high-altitude nuclear tests, the results were inconclusive, in part, due to the surprising results. The newly formed scientific team was determined to be thorough. The result was the implementation of *Operation Fishbowl*.

The *Starfish Prime* test was one of five high-altitude nuclear detonations, conducted as part of *Operation Fishbowl*, a series of tests in 1962 that had begun in direct response to the Soviet announcement on August 30, 1961, that the Soviet Union would end a three-year moratorium on testing. The Starfish Prime test was originally planned as the second in the Operation Fishbowl series, but the first launch, known as *Bluegill*, was lost by the radar-tracking equipment and had to be destroyed in flight.

On July 8, 1962, Honolulu time, at nine seconds after 11 p.m., the Starfish Prime test was successfully detonated at an altitude of two hundred and fifty miles above the Earth's surface. The actual weapon yield came very close to the design yield, approximately 1.4 megatons—equivalent to 1.4 million tons of TNT. The nuclear warhead detonated 13 minutes and 41 seconds after liftoff of the Thor missile from Johnston Island, in a remote part of the Pacific Ocean.

Reports described the explosion as spherical in shape. The resulting shock wave expanded in all directions and created an incredible aurora that was seen as far away as Honolulu, about a thousand miles away from the detonation point. The observing scientists noted that the electrons traveled away from the explosion at incredible speeds, following the Earth's magnetic field, and then dropped into the upper atmosphere. As they collided with the atoms and molecules comprising the Earth's atmosphere, the electrons were absorbed—generating the man-made aurora.

However, the scientists were not there for the light show. When the bomb detonated, the electrons underwent an incredible acceleration, creating a brief, but extremely powerful magnetic field. This was what they were looking for—an electromagnetic pulse. Starfish Prime caused an EMP far greater than expected. The shock wave drove much of the instrumentation off the scale, causing great difficulty in compiling accurate measurements. The Starfish Prime electromagnetic pulse also made those effects known to the unaware public, by causing electrical damage in Hawaii. The strength of the EMP affected the flow of electricity for a thousand miles, knocking out about 300 streetlights, setting off numerous burglar alarms, and damaging a telephone company microwave link. The EMP damage to the microwave link shut down telephone service throughout the Hawaiian Islands.

While the EMP had been predicted by scientists, there was another effect that had not been anticipated. The electrons from the blast didn't descend into the Earth's atmosphere, but instead lingered in space for months. They became trapped by the Earth's magnetic field, creating an artificial radiation belt high above the surface.

The scientists discovered when a high-speed electron collides with a satellite, it could generate a miniature electromagnetic pulse. The net effect was that these electrons could strike satellites and disrupt their electronics. The pulse of electrons from the Starfish Prime detonation damaged at least six satellites, all of which eventually failed due to the blast.

Nuclear scientists around the world were astonished. The size of the pulse generated was not anticipated by anyone. As a result, future tests by the U.S. were conducted with a much lower yield. In a report issued by the Defense Threat Reduction Agency in 2010, the results of the Starfish Prime test were cited as the primary evidence of the threat that an EMP would pose to satellites and other space assets.

PART THREE

PRESENT DAY USE OF EMP
TECHNOLOGY

Early-Time HEMP Mechanism (E1)

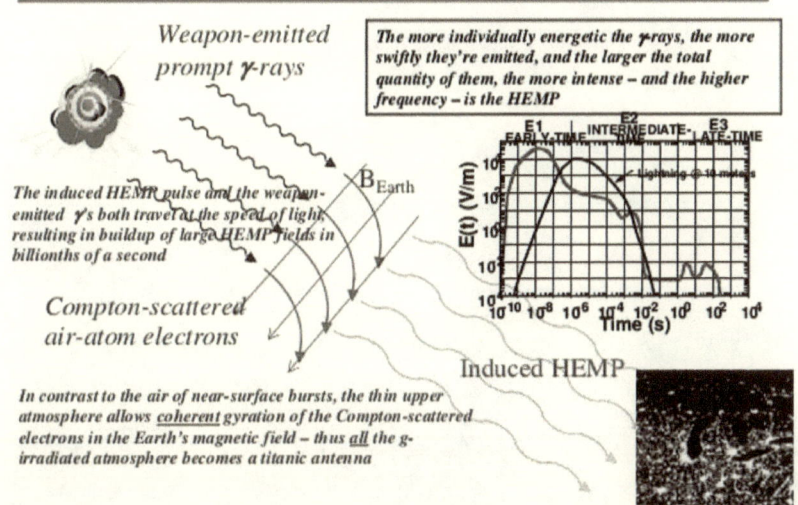

Weapon-emitted prompt γ-rays

The more individually energetic the γ-rays, the more swiftly they're emitted, and the larger the total quantity of them, the more intense – and the higher frequency – is the HEMP

The induced HEMP pulse and the weapon-emitted γ's both travel at the speed of light, resulting in buildup of large HEMP fields in billionths of a second

Compton-scattered air-atom electrons

Induced HEMP

In contrast to the air of near-surface bursts, the thin upper atmosphere allows coherent gyration of the Compton-scattered electrons in the Earth's magnetic field – thus all the g-irradiated atmosphere becomes a titanic antenna

CHAPTER FIVE
RECENT EVENTS IN THE USE OF EMP

Critical infrastructure such as communications, the power grid, economic centers, and transportation routes have always been a primary target in a time of war—both to erode military capabilities and to bring political pressure to bear. The United States is somewhat transparent about the locations of some of the major military and intelligence facilities and key economic nodes are very easy to pinpoint, as well. After all, the 9/11 attackers went after a military target, the Pentagon, and an economic one, the World Trade Center. Also, most U.S. military bases are connected to civilian electricity grids, as are any economic targets, an interdependency that is well known. In this age of electricity, the grid is what the military calls a *center of gravity*. Simply put, a *center of gravity* is a nation's source of power—both politically, and with respect to their critical infrastructure. As a result, EMP weapons have begun to find more practical applications in the top militaries around the world as a tool to breach a nation's vulnerabilities.

During the 1991 Gulf War, the U.S. carried, and used EMP weapons on its E-8 Joint Stars aircraft, to disrupt electronic command systems, which international analysts believe was one of the main advantages that our military enjoyed. The U.S. Navy used EMP weapons on the first day of the Persian Gulf War to destroy electronic defense and communications systems in Iraq. Military and industry sources that were familiar with the military's plan, described a top secret *black program* for the development of the EMP weapon. EMP warheads were carried on a few of the Navy's Tomahawk cruise missiles, which were the ideal delivery system to reach Baghdad.

In March 1999, the U.S. military used microwave weapons during the NATO bombing of Yugoslavia, causing communication in certain areas to be disrupted for more than three hours. This event brought a nuclear dimension to the Balkan War. At the time, Russia was hesitant to ratify the START II treaty. There was the usual political posturing between the U.S. and Russia. After the bombings occurred, reportedly utilizing U.S. B-2 Stealth aircraft, one Russian treaty negotiator quipped, "today Serbia, tomorrow Moscow." Most political observers opined that the use of an EMP-style weapon brought the Russians to the table because of their concerns of future use against their country.

In March 2003, at the start of the Iraq War, EMP weapons were used to sever Iraqi state television broadcast signals. CBS News reported it this way:

"The U.S. Air Force has hit Iraqi TV with an experimental electromagnetic pulse device called the 'E-Bomb' in an attempt to knock it off the air and shut down Saddam Hussein's propaganda machine. The highly classified bomb creates a brief pulse of microwaves powerful enough to fry computers, blind radar, silence radios, trigger crippling power outages and disable the electronic ignitions in vehicles and aircraft.

Iraqi satellite TV, which broadcasts 24 hours a day outside Iraq, went off the air around 4:30 a.m. local time (8:30 p.m. ET Tuesday). Officially, the Pentagon does not acknowledge the weapon's existence. Asked about it at a March 5 news conference at the Pentagon, Gen. Tommy Franks said: "I can't talk to you about that because I don't know anything about it."

CHAPTER SIX
TECHNOLOGICAL ADVANCES; NON-MILITARY USES

Pulsed electromagnetic field therapy (PEMFT), also called pulsed magnetic therapy or pulse magneto therapy, is a technique most commonly used in the area of orthopedics for the treatment of bone fractures, failed bone fusions, and congenital bone fractures. In the case of bone healing, PEMFT uses directed pulsed electromagnetic fields through injured tissue. This electromagnetic pulse stimulates cellular repair. The FDA has approved several such stimulation devices as a solution that may assist in bone repair.

Although electromagnetic therapy became widely adopted in Western Europe, its use was restricted to animals in North America. Veterinarians became the first health professionals to use PEMF therapy, usually to heal broken legs in racehorses. Professional sports doctors then decided to experiment with veterinarian devices on professional athletes that ultimately led to legally licensed devices for human use in the United States – but under strict stipulations that it was only to be used for non-union bone fractures, under a medical prescription from a licensed doctor.

In 1979, the FDA approved non-invasive devices using pulsed electromagnetic fields designed to stimulate bone growth.

In 2004, a pulsed electromagnetic field system was approved by the FDA, as a supplement to cervical fusion surgery in patients at a high risk for non-fusion.

Electromagnetic fields as cutting tools

The bodywork on motor vehicles must be sufficiently stable, but processing the high-strength steels involved -- for example, punching holes in them -- can prove to be something of a challenge. A new steel-cutting process, using electromagnetic fields, has been hailed as a way for automobile manufacturers to save time, energy and money in the future.

Squealing tires and the crunch of impact – when an accident occurs, the steel sheets that form a motor vehicle's bodywork must provide adequate impact protection and shield its passengers to the greatest extent possible. But the strength of the steel creates its own set of challenges; such as when automobile manufacturers have to punch holes in the automobile's body for cable routing. Mechanical cutting tools, struggling to pierce the hard steel, rapidly wear out. Traditional automated tools also leave some waste material on the underside of the steel known as *burr*. Therefore, additional time has to be spent on the finishing process. One possible alternative is to use lasers as cutters, but they require a great deal of energy, which makes the entire process time-consuming and costly.

Working together with several partners, including Volkswagen, researchers at the Fraunhofer Institute in Germany have come up with another way to make holes in press-hardened steel bodywork. Dr. Verena Kräusel, one department head at Fraunhofer explained:

"The new method is based on electromagnetic pulse technology that was previously used primarily to expand aluminum tubes. We've modified it to cut even hard steels. Whereas a laser takes around 1.4 seconds to cut a hole, an EMP can do the job in approximately 200 milliseconds – up to seven times faster. Another advantage is that it produces no burr, thus doing away with the need for a finishing process. Stamping presses become superfluous, and no costs arise from the need to replace worn-out parts."

The electromagnetic pulse generators contain a coil, a capacitor battery, a charging device, and high-current switches. When the switch closes, the capacitors discharge via the coil within a matter of microseconds, producing a high pulsed current. The coil converts the energy stored in the capacitors into magnetic energy. To be able to use this process to cut steel, the researchers simply had to modify the coil to ensure the resulting electromagnetic field was strong enough. The pressure with which the field hit the steel needed to be so high that it forcibly expelled the material from the sheet. Dr. Kräusel likened the impact pressure on the steel to the weight of three small cars on a finger nail.

Electromagnetic Pulse Cannon

For years, law enforcement sought a method to stop an elusive, speeding car without killing its driver and passengers using traditional means, such as bullets. Even if a skilled sniper can fire a disabling shot into a car's engine block, loss of life is probable. But Eureka Aerospace, a Canadian company, announced in 2014 the development of an electromagnetic pulse cannon capable of destroying an automobile's electronic ignition and computer system.

The EMP cannon utilizes a suitcase-sized antenna that weighs roughly fifty pounds and is designed to stop cars in their tracks up to seven hundred feet away. According to scientists at Eureka, the disabling power would only work for post-1970 vehicles that rely upon microprocessors and various electronics for their operation.

Electromagnetic Propulsion

The principles discovered in nuclear EMP testing resulted in the development of electromagnetic propulsion, which is the principle of accelerating an object by the utilization of a flowing electrical current and magnetic fields. The electrical current is used to either create an opposing magnetic field or to charge a fluid, which can then be repelled. When a current is discharged through a conductor in a magnetic field, an electromagnetic influence known as a Lorentz force pushes the conductor in a direction perpendicular to the magnetic field. This repulsing force is what causes propulsion in a system that is designed to take advantage of the phenomenon. One key difference between EMP and propulsion achieved by electric motors, is that the electrical energy used for EMP is not used to produce rotational energy for motion; though both use magnetic fields and a flowing electrical current.

Space Technologies

There are multiple applications for EMP technologies in the field of aerospace. One is the use of EMP technology to control orbiting satellites. These systems are based on the direct interactions between the vehicle's electromagnetic field and the magnetic field of the Earth. The advantages of EMP designed systems are the very precise and instantaneous control over the satellite's responsiveness. Also, the expected electrical efficiencies are far greater than those of current chemical rockets that attain propulsion through the use of heat which results in low fuel efficiencies and significant amounts of gaseous pollutants.

CHAPTER SEVEN
MILITARY USES

Weapons of Electromagnetic Mass Destruction

Fighting a War Across the Electromagnetic Spectrum (EMS)

Recently, the Pentagon has made a significant effort to showcase its budding cyber warfare capabilities. But the military has been less forthcoming about an essential, more substantial component of their military capabilities — electromagnetic warfare – until recently.

The use of electromagnetic pulse technology is one of the most critical operational tools in modern warfare, but its use in military operations is rapidly changing. EMS operations can be roughly broken down into communications, sensing, and electromagnetic warfare. Most people are familiar with communication and sensing systems, such as radios and radar in the radio frequency portion of the EMS. In the future, military systems will use a wider rangeswath of the EMS, including capabilities that use laser light, infrared (IR) and ultraviolet (UV) radiation, or emitters and detectors that radiate in the X-ray and gamma-ray regions of the spectrum.

The term *electronic warfare* refers to the use of electromagnetic energy and directed energy to attack an enemy's capabilities. The Department of Defense divides electronic warfare operations into three broad categories:

Electronic attack, involves the use of electromagnetic pulse technology-based weaponry to attack facilities or equipment with the intent of degrading, neutralizing, or destroying enemy combat capability.

Electronic protection, which refers to actions taken to protect personnel, facilities, and equipment from the effects of friendly, neutral, or enemy use of an EMP, as well as to naturally occurring phenomena that degrade, neutralize, or destroy friendly combat capability.

Electronic warfare support, which includes actions to identify and locate sources of intentional and unintentional, radiated EMP energy.

The Army just publically released its first-ever Field Manual for Cyber – Electromagnetic Activities. This manual covers operations related to cyberspace and the electromagnetic spectrum, highlighting that electromagnetic warfare is as important as the threat of cyber warfare.

The Army's field manual describes a variety of options in its use of electronic warfare, or EW. The tools at the military's disposal range from sending confusing signals and messages that degrade the enemy's communications capability on the battlefield, to finding enemy equipment and destroying it with an electromagnetic pulse. The manual does not explain how to conduct specific EW attacks, but it does guide soldiers on what these sorts of operations look like regarding protocol, terminology, command and control. The military recognizes the number of potential electronic warfare operations is growing with every new radio or internet-dependent device that the military acquires.

With its use of electromagnetic pulse weaponry, the military can impact the ability to fly a drone, use GPS, or even drop a smart bomb, but EMP technology doesn't just represent a weapon for use by the U.S. military. It's also a potential vulnerability. The U.S. does not have a monopoly on the use of electromagnetic pulse technology. In the last few years, off-the-shelf pieces of wireless communications equipment have allowed everyone, from hobbyists to terrorists, to access the electromagnetic spectrum efficiently, in the form of radio frequency weapons.

The importance of this technology stimulated the Army to establish a new career field dedicated to electronic warfare in 2009. Unfortunately, like so many other aspects of our military, our reliance on electromagnetic pulse technology might be growing faster than our ability to keep defending against it.

Our military is scrambling to develop new tools and techniques that will help it preserve its electromagnetic edge, but that advantage continues to shrink. Soon, our inability to completely control the spectrum might result in a different kind of war as weapons of electromagnetic mass destruction proliferate.

As stated in *Cyber Warfare*, the electromagnetic pulse capability will go hand-in-hand with newly developed cyber operations. While there are definite similarities, cyber operations have a broader range of capacities than the traditional EMP strategic role, and can support a wider range of operations. Defensively, counter-EMP techniques have a more limited scope than the huge needs to defend our military and critical infrastructure from cyber attacks.

Electronic warfare and cyber warfare are closely related and should be treated as such. The overlap between electronic operations related to drones, communications, and improvised explosive devices on the battlefield, and cyber warfare—which we commonly think of as being about ones, zeros, and hackers, shows our Pentagon is evolving in its view of both fields.

For U.S. soldiers, according to the current approach by our military, electronic and cyber warfare are the same. Eventually, the term cyber or electronic war may become obsolete. It might be time just to call it war. As Albert Einstein wrote:

I know not with what weapons WW3 will be fought, but WW4 will be fought with sticks and stones.

The Impact of Defense Department Budget Cuts

The Defense Department may be facing some of the most significant budget cuts in decades, but many are confident that the Pentagon will develop new cost-effective, and efficient, technologies to fight our enemies.

Speaking at a Bloomberg Government in 2015, research and development leaders from the U.S. Armed Forces all identified their top *game-changing* technologies.

Rear Adm. Matthew Klunder, the chief of naval research, suggested that directed energy via electromagnetic pulse technology— electromagnetic railguns, lasers, and microwaves—

would all be significant developments that could place the United States ahead of potential threats.

He said that the USS Ponce, which had an operational, directed energy laser cannon on board, that would fire the weapon at a cost of less than $1 per round. It could be used to take out potential threats, such as an Iranian drones and swarm boats, utilizing its lethal to non-lethal energy spectrum.

A concern of many DOD watchers is that budget cuts could cripple the U.S. military's hopes for maintaining supremacy in research and technology. One can only hope that the Secretary of Defense will not relinquish our nation's technological advantage and innovation to the Russians or Chinese.

Limitations of EMP Weapons

The limitations of electromagnetic weapons are determined by weapon implementation, means of delivery, and administration policy concerning rules of engagement. Weapon application will determine the electromagnetic field strength achievable at a given radius, and its spectral distribution. Means of delivery will constrain the accuracy with which the weapon can be positioned in relation to the intended target. Both constrain lethality. Rules of engagement can only be determined by a particular administration's foreign policy and defense goals.

In the context of targeting military equipment, it must be noted that vacuum tube equipment is substantially more resilient to the electromagnetic weapons effects than solid state, transistor technology. Therefore, a hard electrical kill may not be achieved against targets using antiquated technology.

Means of delivery will limit the lethality of an electromagnetic bomb by introducing limits to the weapon's size and the accuracy of its delivery. Advanced technology, as discussed below, is addressing this issue.

Politically, the accuracy of delivery and achievable lethal radius must be considered against the acceptable collateral damage for the chosen target. Where collateral electrical damage or significant human impact is a consideration, accuracy of delivery and lethal radius are critical parameters. An inaccurately delivered weapon with a large lethal radius may be unusable against a target, should the likely collateral electrical damage be beyond acceptable limits. Collateral damage may be a major issue for nation-states constrained by restrictive rules of engagement designed to avoid unexpected loss of life.

Railgun Applications

Electromagnetic railguns -- that use electricity rather than chemical propellants to launch projectiles -- are potential game changers too. There are currently two working prototypes under consideration at the Marine Corps Base at Quantico. At $25,000 per round, the electromagnetic railgun may be capable of the same results as multimillion-dollar missiles.

Railguns are of particular interest to the military, as an alternative to current bulky artillery. Railgun ammunition, in the form of small tungsten missiles, would be relatively light, simple to transport, and easy to handle. Due to their high velocities, railgun missiles would be less susceptible to bullet drop and wind shift, than current artillery shells. Course correction would be important, but all missiles fired from railgun artillery could be guided by satellite.

It would be harder to engineer small arms railguns, mainly because of recoil. Recoil, the backward action of a firearm upon discharge, is determined by the momentum of the escaping projectile. Multiplying a projectile's mass by its velocity yields its momentum, which for high-velocity railgun projectiles, would be considerable. A portable railgun that fires very small bullets may be the solution. A small bullet would limit recoil, but still carry enough kinetic energy to inflict severe damage.

Railguns have also been proposed as important components of the Strategic Defense Initiative, popularly known as Star Wars. Star Wars is a U.S. government program responsible for the research and development of a space-based system to defend the nation from attack by strategic ballistic missiles. Railguns could fire projectiles to intercept the incoming missiles. Some scientists argue that railguns could also protect Earth from rogue asteroids, by firing high-velocity projectiles from orbit. Upon impact, the projectiles would either destroy the incoming asteroid or change its trajectory.

Railguns have some interesting non-military applications as well. For one thing, they could potentially launch satellites or space shuttles into the upper atmosphere, where auxiliary rockets would kick in. On bodies without an atmosphere, such as the moon, railguns could deliver projectiles to space without chemical propellant, which would require air to function.

Railguns could also be used to initiate fusion reactions. Fusion occurs when two small atomic nuclei combine to form a larger nucleus, a process that releases large amounts of energy. Atomic nuclei must be traveling at enormous velocities for this to happen. Some scientists propose using railguns to fire pellets of fusible material at each other. The impact of the high-velocity pellets would create immense temperatures and pressures, enabling fusion to occur.

With continued successes such as these, the railgun may one day be the weapon of choice on the battlefield and the propellant of choice on the launch pad.

MAHEM: MAgneto Hydrodynamic Explosive Munition

Small drones are the ultimate smart bombs. They are potentially portable, personal cruise missiles capable of putting a warhead on target, miles away. Some, like the Israeli Hero-30, are already being deployed. But the next generation of such U.S. weapons will have advanced warheads that can hit targets from tanks to buildings. These will be based on a railgun weapons technology, descriptively known as MAHEM.

With the prospect of railguns replacing heavy artillery, scientists began to focus their efforts on the use of electromagnetic pulse technology in advanced weaponry. The railgun uses electromagnetic force to drive a projectile to phenomenal speeds impossible with gunpowder-style propulsion. With MAHEM, or MAgnetoHydrodynamic Explosive Munition, you could carry the same sort of power in your hand because it weighs about five pounds.

Since 2008, the Pentagon, in conjunction with DARPA, the

Defense Advanced Research Projects Agency, placed MAHEM into a weapons development program. At the time of this writing, virtually all information about the program is classified—at least, all information from the U.S. government. Unfortunately, most of the details surrounding the MAHEM program can be found online at a somewhat surprising source—China. The Chinese, known for their use of cyber warfare to steal our military secrets, may be reverse-engineering this advanced weapons technology.

The Evolution of Warheads

Explosive warheads have worked in pretty much the same way since Henry Shrapnel's 1784 artillery shell, which was designed to explode and throw out musket balls in all directions. The shaped charge was a 20th-century refinement in which the force of the explosion blasted a hollow metal cone into an armor-piercing jet, enabling low-velocity weapons like the bazooka to knock out heavy tanks. A newer technology, the explosively formed projectile, arrived on the scene. Here, the explosion folds the metal into an aerodynamic slug that is less penetrating than a shaped charge, but able to do more damage against lightly-armored targets. Since it's a larger mass at a lower velocity, it makes a bigger hole.

MAHEM is different because it combines explosives with electricity. It works in three stages. The first stage is an electronically modified explosion. The explosion creates an expanding fireball; applying an electrical pulse to the fireball, which increases the velocity and pressure of the blast wave. The addition of the electromagnetic pulse adds to the size and duration of the impact.

In the second stage, the power of the explosion is transitioned into electricity. This builds on previous weapons testing that convert explosive power into an electromagnetic pulse. In MAHEM, a ceramic material produces an intense electric current as the shockwave hits it, in a process known as electromagnetic braking. In contrast to a typical explosion, in which most of the energy is wasted, scientists claim MAHEM has superb energy conversion efficiency.

MAHEM technology has been developing slowly. It came to the public's attention in 2008, when DARPA's plans for the next year included, "develop and conduct experiments to demonstrate the feasibility of a self-contained MAHEM in the form of an AT4 shoulder-mounted munition," (The AT4 is a small bazooka used by the US Army with a one-pound warhead). This amazing-sounding weapons tech got a flurry of attention back then, including mentions in *Popular Mechanics,* and was a popular weapon of choice in the video game *Call of Duty.*

Then, MAHEM disappeared from the public radar.

There is little information available, just a few tantalizing mentions in Pentagon documents of how the technology is coming along. A look at the Small Business Administration's SBIR program—Small Business Innovation Research, reveals contract funding for several MAHEM related projects. One research project is investigating a dial-a-yield warhead that could be set to any blast level as needed. Another is a contract for the *Novel Light-weight Warhead for Breaching and Destroying Hardened Structures*— a shoulder-launched bunker-buster that was completed last year. The latest version is the Electromagnetic Explosive Warhead (EMEW), a MAHEM warhead for the US Army's Organic Precision Munitions program, which includes portable lethal drones. According to SBIR.com, EMEW provides *augmented explosion, selectable fragmentation, and controlled blast.* The pattern and direction of the effects are controllable enabling it to produce a blast wave with no fragments, like a giant stun grenade, to achieve non-lethal effects. The non-lethal effects comport with the Obama administration's stated rules of engagement.

It is difficult to find information online about MAHEM. DARPA representatives claim their MAHEM program ended by 2013. Some online sources indicate the development is now under the auspices of the Army Research Laboratory. The veil of secrecy by the Pentagon looks like an attempt to prevent any technical details of MAHEM from getting out. The Pentagon may have underestimated the ability of the Chinese to conduct *cyber research*, with that term used loosely.

One source revealed a research document entitled, *Physical Modeling of Magneto Hydrodynamic Explosive Munition and Detonation Control.* The study was undertaken by the ministerial key laboratory at the Nanjing

University of Science and Technology, one of the oldest and most prestigious institutions of education in China. The researchers describe, in some detail, how MAHEM works. This information appears to be based on the reverse-engineering of MAHEM by the Chinese scientists.

China is by far the world's largest producer of commercial drones, selling over a half a million this year, including popular models like the Phantom III. It is a small step from there to building small military drones, and MAHEM could take the striking power of small drones to another level.

If Pentagon watchers are accurate, MAHEM will be more effective than existing anti-tank weaponry while also being deadly against other targets, including small buildings, armed pick-up trucks, and electronics targeted by drone strikes.

CHAMP by Boeing

A recent weapons flight test in the Utah desert may change future warfare after the missile successfully defeated electronic targets with little to no collateral damage.

Boeing and the U.S. Air Force Research Laboratory situated at Kirtland Air Force Base, in New Mexico, successfully tested the Counter-electronics High-powered Microwave Advanced Missile

Project —*CHAMP*, during a flight over the Utah Test and Training Range.

CHAMP, which renders electronic targets useless via an electromagnetic pulse, is a non-kinetic alternative to traditional explosive.

During the test, the CHAMP missile navigated a pre-programmed flight plan and emitted bursts of high-powered energy, effectively knocking out the target's data and electronic subsystems. CHAMP allows for selective high-frequency radio wave strikes against numerous targets during a single mission.

"This technology marks a new era in modern-day warfare," said Keith Coleman, CHAMP program manager for Boeing Phantom Works. "In the near future, this technology may be used to render an enemy's electronic and data systems useless even before the first troops or aircraft arrive."

The action of the high-power microwave had the same effect as an electromagnetic pulse. A cruise missile, which was launched from a U.S. bomber, was pre-programmed to fly over a target and shoot a burst of high-power microwaves at a two-story building. It knocked out rows of personal computers and electrical systems that were shown in a video taken of the test. Following the first target, the cruise missile, then was guided to six other targets, resulting in knocking out all electronics.

The effects of a CHAMP are very similar to what would happen during an electromagnetic pulse caused by a high-altitude nuclear detonation or by a powerful solar storm, just on a much smaller, more focused scale. Unlike an EMP bomb, which are area weapons and indiscriminate as to who they target within their blast area, CHAMP is an EMP assassin that comes in and surgically eliminates an enemy's war enabling technology, barely leaving a trace that it was there.

JASSM-ER by Raytheon

The AGM-158 JASSM (Joint Air-to-Surface Standoff Missile) is a long-range missile developed and produced by Lockheed Martin. This conventional, air-to-ground and precision standoff missile was designed primarily for the U.S. Air Force. The one-ton class weapon offers high capability and precision in destroying stationary, as well as mobile targets.

The JASSM, and the extended range version, JASSM-ER, have the flexibility to be integrated into various platforms such as B-1, B-2, B-52, F-16, and F-15E aircraft and is currently deployed on Australia's F/A-18A/B aircraft and Finland's F/A-18 C/D aircraft. It offers enhanced survivability, lethality, and a long-range precision strike to the warfighter, during day and night operations.

The JASSM flies automatically through a predetermined route by using the onboard navigation system that includes an Anti-Jam Global Positioning System.

CHAMP has cleared all of the necessary hurdles for deployment, so it needs a proper platform for use against the enemy. JASSM-ER is a logical platform for CHAMP, as it can be launched by both bombers and fighters, and is a proven design that has already evolved into a highly advanced anti-ship missile. Also, it is smart and stealthy, able to actively detect threatening radars, and evade or attack them, making it survivable against the world's most capable air defense systems.

Conclusions

Electromagnetic bombs are *weapons of electrical mass destruction* with applications across a broad spectrum of targets, spanning both the strategic and tactical. The use of EMP technology in advanced weaponry offers a very high payoff in attacking the fundamental information processing and communication facilities of an adversary. The massed application of these weapons will produce physical paralysis in any target system, thus providing a decisive advantage in the conduct of electronic warfare.

EMP weaponry can cause hard electrical kills over larger areas than conventional explosive weapons of similar mass. Also, they offer substantial economies in force size for a given level of inflicted damage and are thus a potent force multiplier for appropriate targets. The non-lethal nature of electromagnetic weapons makes their use far less politically damaging than that of conventional munitions, and therefore, broadens the range of military options available.

It is incumbent upon Washington, to appreciate both the offensive and defensive implications of electromagnetic pulse technology. Failure to consider the consequences of the proliferation of EMP technology, and to take measures to safeguard our vital assets and critical infrastructure from possible future attack, could be catastrophic for the Unites States.

PART FOUR
THE THREAT IS REAL

Chapter Eight
Components of a Credible EMP Attack

Based upon what we know, could AN EMP bring down the U.S. Power Grid?

A high-altitude electromagnetic pulse (HEMP) attack upon our nation's critical infrastructure would have devastating consequences for the U.S.

Such an attack would have the effect of collapsing the electric grid and other critical infrastructure for months or years, including unprotected military and civilian electronics. The U.S. missile defense system is capable of defending against a nuclear missile from the north. If such an attack were to come from the south, we would be unprepared, according to experts. Iran is regarded as already having nuclear missiles capable of making an EMP attack against the U.S. North Korea is rapidly developing orbiting satellites that could potentially launch an EMP attack from space. Recently, critical NORAD operations have been moving back into Cheyenne Mountain, which is EMP hardened.

While this is considered prudent, the American people are largely unprotected from the ramifications. It's estimated that in the event of a yearlong nationwide blackout, ninety percent of Americans would perish from starvation, disease, and societal chaos, according to members of the Congressional EMP Commission, which published its last unclassified report in 2008, the executive summary of which is found in Appendix C.

Experts claim that the Obama Administration has not acted on the EMP Commission's proposed executive order to protect national infrastructure considered essential, to provide for defense against an EMP attack. Hardening the national electric grid would cost several billion dollars, an insignificant amount when compared to the potential loss of life following an EMP attack. Congress has also failed to act on the recommendations of its own EMP commission, to protect the electric grid and other civilian infrastructure that depend on a viable electric grid—such as communications, transportation, and banking—that are essential to the economy. Several bills have gained bipartisan support in the House but died in the Senate. Fortunately, states are not waiting for the federal government, with Texas being among the states that have an initiative underway to deal with an EMP attack.

As is often the case, legislation gets caught up in the politics, and lack of action on the EMP Commission's recommendations is no exception. Over the past decade, there has been an ongoing debate over whether the threat posed by an EMP is real. This debate heated up in 2015 when bipartisan support arose for a national commitment to address the EMP threat, by hardening the national infrastructure.

There is little doubt that efforts by the United States to harden its utilities against EMP — and its ability to manage critical infrastructure manually in the event of an EMP attack — have been eroded in recent decades, as the Cold War ended and the threat of nuclear conflict with Russia lessened. This is also true of the U.S. military, which has spent little time contemplating such scenarios in the years since the fall of the Soviet Union. The cost of remedying the situation, especially retrofitting older systems, is immense. As with any issue involving massive amounts of money, the debate over guarding against an EMP attack has become quite politicized in recent years.

Gauging the Threat of an Electromagnetic Pulse Attack

To determine whether the threat is real, we must discuss the tactical elements involved in an EMP attack and which nation-states are capable of launching such an attack. The following is our assessment of the likelihood of an EMP attack against the United States.

The effects of an EMP have the potential to be quite significant, but they are also quite uncertain. Despite the meaningful amount of testing undertaken in the late 1950's into the early 60's, test data from high-altitude nuclear explosions is extremely limited. The U.S. and the Soviet Union conducted less than twenty atmospheric nuclear tests above twelve miles. The widespread effects of a high-altitude nuclear detonation above this height are unknown.

In 1963, after the Partial Test Ban Treaty went into effect, prohibiting its signatories from conducting aboveground test detonations and ending atmospheric tests — scientists still questioned the effects of a high-altitude EMP. The Starfish Prime test of 1962 was not designed to study HEMP, and the effect on Hawaii, which was so far from ground zero, startled U.S. scientists. High-altitude nuclear testing effectively ended before the parameters and effects of HEMP were well understood. The limited body of knowledge that was gained from these tests remains highly classified in both the U.S. and Russia.

Despite these uncertainties, the importance of the EMP threat should not be understated. There is no doubt that the impact of a HEMP attack would be significant. But any nation-state plotting such an attack would be dealing with immense uncertainties — not only about the ideal altitude at which to detonate the device, based on its design and yield to maximize its effect, but also about the nature of those effects and just how devastating they would be.

Non-nuclear devices that create an EMP-like effect, such as high-power microwave devices, and radio frequency weapons, are now available to several countries, including the U.S. The most capable of these devices are portable and have significant tactical utility. The technology is still developing, and more powerful variants may be able to achieve greater effects on specific targets.

But at present, non-nuclear electromagnetic pulse weapons do not appear to be able to create an EMP effect large enough to affect an entire city, much less a country. Because of this, we will confine our discussion of the EMP threat caused by a high-altitude nuclear detonation, which also happens to be the most prevalent scenario causing concern in Washington.

Components of a Credible HEMP Threat

For there to be a credible HEMP threat, five things are needed:

- The delivery mechanism to reach the required altitude

- A sophisticated nuclear warhead for the missile to deliver

- A motive for conducting an EMP attack

- A suitable target for maximum desired effect

- The absence of a deterrent or responsive counter-attack

The question then becomes: Who is capable of carrying out the threat?

Plausible HEMP Attack Scenarios

To have the best chance of causing the type of widespread EMP damage to the continental U.S., a nuclear weapon carrying a one megaton payload would need to be detonated approximately twenty miles above the Earth's surface, somewhere over the central part of the country. Modern commercial aircraft normally cruise at a third of this altitude. To achieve the desired height, a nation-state would require both the requisite warhead design and intercontinental ballistic missile (ICBM) capability, to conduct such an attack from their territory. The UK, France, Russia and China have all possessed this ability for decades. Although shorter range missiles can achieve this altitude, the center of the U.S. is still a thousand miles from the east or west coast. One of the biggest concerns of the Pentagon, is the use of a shorter range missile fired from a freighter that enters the Gulf of Mexico. In recent years, North Korea has passed several large commercial vessels, through the Panama Canal towards Cuba, virtually undetected with nuclear missiles in their hold. It is less than eight hundred miles from the Gulf of Mexico to St. Louis, Missouri—the heartland of America.

The HEMP threat has existed since the early 1960s, when nuclear weapons were first paired with ballistic missiles, and necessarily grew to be an important component of the U.S. nuclear strategy. The doctrine of *Mutually Assured Destruction* has prevented the use of HEMP in modern warfare.

Despite the limited understanding of its effects, undoubtedly the U.S., China, and Russia, almost certainly included the use of weapons to create HEMPs in both defensive, and especially offensive scenarios.

However, nuclear weapons have not been employed in an attack anywhere, since 1945. Some pundits believe that a HEMP attack might be considered less destructive, and therefore, less likely to provoke a devastating retaliatory response. Such an attack against the United States would inherently and conclusively represent a nuclear attack on the U.S. homeland, and the idea that the United States would not respond in kind is absurd. The United States continues to maintain the most credible and survivable nuclear deterrent in the world, and any country or terrorist group contemplating a HEMP attack, would have to assume that a reprisal would be full, swift, and devastating. The idea that Washington will interpret the use of a nuclear weapon to create a HEMP, as somehow less hostile than the utilization of a nuclear weapon to physically destroy an American city, is not something a country is likely to gamble on.

Countries that build HEMP weapons invest vast amounts of capital in their nuclear programs. A successful nuclear weapons program is the product of decades of scientific research and development. U.S. nuclear weapons are maintained as a deterrent to an attack, not with the intention of using them offensively. Over the years, the U.S. has achieved an initial first-strike capability. The focus of the Department of Defense is to establish a survivable deterrent that can withstand first, a conventional, and then, a nuclear first strike. Under this policy, the nuclear arsenal can serve its primary purpose as a deterrent, and then a means of counter-attack.

It is comforting to know that the countries capable of carrying out a HEMP attack, still govern themselves by the *Mutually Assured Destruction* doctrine. The principles of nuclear deterrence, and the threat of a full-scale retaliatory strike, continue to hold and govern post-Cold War.

The Threat from Rogue Actors

One of the scenarios that concern Washington is that the EMP threat stems from a rogue state or a terrorist group like ISIS that does not possess ICBMs, but who will use deception to accomplish its mission. A rogue state, like North Korea or Iran, or even a terrorist group, could load a nuclear warhead and missile launcher aboard a cargo ship or tanker. The missile could be launched from our coastal waters, placing the warhead in position for a targeted HEMP strike. This scenario, without leaving any fingerprints, would involve either a short-range ballistic missile to achieve a localized metropolitan strike or a longer-range—but not necessarily intercontinental—ballistic missile to reach the necessary position over the central U.S. to deliver a continental strike.

This threat scenario faces the same obstacles as any other potential nuclear weapon employed in a terrorist attack. It is unlikely that a terrorist group like al Qaeda or Hezbollah can develop a nuclear weapons program. Their organizations do not have the requisite financial or personnel resources to do soit.

It is also highly unlikely that a nation like Iran or North Korea, who have devoted significant resources to developing a nuclear weapon, would entrust such a weapon to an outside terrorist organization. There have been great strides made in the last decade in the field of nuclear forensics. The use of a nuclear weapon would be vigorously investigated, and the nation that produced the weapon would be identified.

A group like ISIS, however, would likely use a nuclear device, if it could obtain one. The risk of a terrorist group acquiring a nuclear capability of any kind, crude or sophisticated is possible, but not likely. Here's why:

The development of a HEMP nuclear weapon requires significant financial resources, scientific talent, and time. An attack scenario from a rogue actor requires a sophisticated nuclear warhead capable of being mated with a ballistic missile. There are considerable technical barriers that separate a crude nuclear device from a sophisticated nuclear warhead.

The engineering expertise required to construct such a warhead is far greater than that needed to build a radio frequency weapon, for example. A warhead must be far more compact than a simple device. It must also have a trigger mechanism and electronics capable of withstanding the force of an ICBM launch, the journey into the cold vacuum of space and the heat and force of re-entering the atmosphere — and still function as designed. Designing a functional warhead takes considerable advances in several fields of science, including physics, electronics, engineering, metallurgy, and explosives technology. Overseeing it all must be a high-end quality assurance capability.

But even if a terrorist organization were able to obtain a functional warhead and compatible fissile core, the challenges of mating the warhead to a missile that it was not designed for, and then getting it to launch and detonate properly, would be far more daunting than it would appear at first glance. Additionally, the process of fueling a liquid-fueled ballistic missile at sea and then launching it from a ship, using an improvised launcher, would also be very challenging. Experts say that North Korea, Iran, and Pakistan all rely heavily on Scud technology, which uses highly volatile, corrosive, and toxic fuels.

Such a scenario is challenging enough, even before the uncertainty of achieving the desired HEMP effect, is taken into account. This is just the kind of complexity and uncertainty that well-trained terrorist operatives seek to avoid in an operation. A ground-level nuclear detonation in a city, such as New York or Washington, would be more likely to cause the type of terror, death, and physical destruction that is sought in a terrorist attack, than could be achieved by a non-lethal EMP. Because of this, it would be far simpler for a terrorist group looking to conduct a nuclear attack to do so using a device such as a Radio Frequency Weapon, than it would be using a sophisticated warhead.

Make no mistake: the threat of an EMP attack is real. Modern civilization depends heavily on electronics and the electrical grid for a broad range of vital functions, and this is truer in the United States, than in most other countries. A HEMP attack or a substantial geomagnetic storm could have a dramatic impact on modern life in the affected area. However, as we've discussed, the EMP threat has been around for more than half a century. Despite the fact that there are some technical and practical variables that make a HEMP attack using a nuclear warhead highly unlikely, rogue nations are working diligently to obtain the technology. When considering the EMP threat, it is important to recognize that it exists as one of many threats, including related threats such as conventional nuclear warfare and targeted, small-scale RFW attacks. The world is a dangerous place, full of potential threats. Some things are more likely to occur than others. As a nation, there is only a limited amount of funding to monitor, harden against, try to prepare for, and manage them all. It is easy to fall into the trap of attempting to defend against everything, although the practical result is that Washington's ineptitude will end up defending against nothing. Focused and rational prioritization of the threats we face as a nation is essential to the country's defense.

Hardening national infrastructure against an EMP—whether man-made or naturally occurring solar flares, is undoubtedly necessary. The country is beginning to open its eyes to the fact that there are very real weaknesses and vulnerabilities in America's critical infrastructure — not to mention in our society overall. Our political leaders must strike a delicate balance between focusing on this very real threat, and spending resources on other potential collapse events.

CHAPTER NINE
THE PLAYERS

Who is capable of carrying out the threat?

We have now established that the nuclear EMP threat is not merely theoretical–it is a clear and present danger. A nuclear EMP attack is the perfect asymmetric weapon for state actors who wish to level the battlefield by neutralizing the great technological advantage enjoyed by the U.S. military forces. EMP is also the only means whereby rogue states or terrorists could use a single nuclear weapon to destroy the United States, and prevail with a single blow.

Russia, China, North Korea, and Iran have already incorporated EMP attacks into their military doctrines, and openly describe making EMP attacks against the United States.

Rogue states and terrorists could use any type of missile, including short-range missiles that can deliver a nuclear warhead, to exact a catastrophic EMP attack on the United States. Iran has tested ship-launched EMP attacks using Scud missiles. Scud, a series of tactical ballistic missiles developed by the Soviet Union during the Cold War, is now in the possession of a dozen countries, including Vietnam, Syria, Libya, and Yemen.

The capabilities of other nations' technologies have grown in the last several years, resulting in an increased likelihood that our enemies could develop advanced EMP weaponry. It is widely known that both Russia and China already have this capability. Now, Iran and North Korea may not be that far behind. Iran, for example, is believed to have simulated a nuclear EMP attack several years ago, using short-range missiles launched from a freighter. Meanwhile, analysts claim that North Korea has acquired the blueprints to build an EMP warhead, possibly from Iran or China.

In July of 2013, a North Korean freighter attempted to pass through the Panama Canal undetected from the Gulf of Mexico with two nuclear-capable missiles in its hold. Three months earlier, in April of 2013, the *Chong Chon Gang* vessel stopped sending its tracking signal to the Automatic Identification System, used worldwide by seagoing vessels. On May 31, it suddenly reappeared on the AIS. The day after, it passed through the Panama Canal and once again, disappeared from the AIS system for forty-five days.

The irregularities of the ship's travel caused Panamanian officials to seize the ship as it attempted to go back to North Korea via the Panama Canal. There was a violent confrontation between the North Korean crew and the Panamanian officials trying to inspect the ship. When the ship was ordered to anchor, the North Korean crew refused. The crew attempted to sabotage the ship by cutting cables on the cranes that would be used to unload the cargo.

When the crew refused to raise anchor and move the vessel as instructed, the authorities were forced to cut the anchor loose. Immediately, a struggle ensued during which the captain of the *Chong Chon Gang* feinted a heart attack and then attempted to commit suicide.

The Panamanian seizure revealed the following cargo:

- 240 metric tons of weapons

- Russian designed Radar/Control systems for missile launching

- Two Russian-made MiG-21 aircraft

- Plane engines and motors

- Live munitions and ordnance, including the parts needed to make two nuclear-capable missiles.

Both Iran and North Korea have been actively pursuing nuclear EMP weaponry. They have successfully orbited a number of satellites that could evade U.S. early warning radars. If these orbiting satellites are carrying nuclear warheads, they could easily deliver a HEMP to the proper altitude to impact the entire continental U.S.

The North Korean example illustrates the warning issued by Defense Secretary Donald Rumsfeld in 2002. He said, "At any given time, there's any number off our coast—coming, going, on transporter-erector-launchers, and they simply erect it, fire off a ballistic missile, put it down, cover it up. Their radar signature is not any different than fifty others in close proximity."

Capability + Desire > The Inverse Relationship

As we wrote in *Cyber Warfare*, there is an inverse relationship between the capability to launch, and successfully detonate, a nuclear delivered EMP weapon and the desire to do so.

CHINA
China leads the way in EMP research and application

While China calls the potential use of an EMP weapon against U.S. interests its *ace*, officials inside the Department of Defense have declared such a threat to be *reckless and irresponsible*. Further, the Chinese military has publicly stated their intentions to use a nuclear EMP as part of a *one-two punch* to knock out all defensive electronics of its adversaries, including Taiwan or any U.S. military assets in the region.

In response, the Department of Defense attempted to quell the threatened use of an EMP by China. Reports quoted an unnamed source as saying, "the Department is unaware of any increase in the threat of a deliberate destructive use of an EMP device. Further, any reporting to the contrary by those without access to current threat assessments is both reckless and irresponsible."

But even the Department of Defense has admitted that our country's intelligence resources lack the technical means to monitor the development of the nuclear weapons programs of other nations, or terrorist organizations. Working in concert with the Defense Science Board, a committee of civilian experts appointed to advise the Defense Department on the growing threat of biological, chemical, and nuclear weaponry, the DOD has placed a greater emphasis on defense strategies for advanced ballistic and cruise missile threats that carry a HEMP payload.

The report of the DSB, whose civilian members hold high-security clearances, warned that there has been an increase in the capabilities of existing nuclear states, especially China, and a horizontal proliferation in the number of states and non-state actors possessing or attempting to possess nuclear weapons. These factors led the DSB to observe that monitoring for proliferation should be a top national security objective.

Shashoujian: China's *Assassin's Mace* Concept

China's military is developing electromagnetic pulse weapons that Beijing plans to use against U.S. aircraft carriers in any future conflict over Taiwan, or its expansion into the South China Sea. The lethal effects of electromagnetic pulse and high-powered microwave weapons revealed are part of China's *shashoujian*, or *assassin's mace* arsenal—weapons that allow a technologically inferior China to level the playing field with U.S. military forces.

Microwave weapons could be used to shut down enemy radar, communications, computers and other electronics, in an opening salvo. The weapons also could jam electronics of attacking aircraft and anti-radiation missiles, and as an anti-satellite weapon, degrade sensitive satellite electronics systems. Pentagon reports on China's military in the past, made only passing references to the *assassin's mace* arsenal. China and Taiwan have been at odds politically for sixty-five years. For years, Beijing has continuously threatened to bring the Taiwanese under its control using military force, or otherwise. For use against Taiwan, China could detonate at an EMP at a relatively low altitude of twenty miles to confine the EMP effects to Taiwan, and minimize damage to electronics on China's mainland. As the Chinese military seeks an advantage in the area of EMP warfare, the world has taken notice. According to reports, China boasts that its *assassin's mace* electronic weapons are part of a trump card, based on unique, new technology *that has been developed in high secrecy*. Experts believe the *trump card* would be useful if the Chinese have developed new low-yield, possibly enhanced, EMP warheads.

According to analysts, China recently conducted EMP tests on mice, rats, rabbits, dogs, and monkeys, that produce eye, brain, bone marrow, and other organ injuries. It's clear that the real purpose of the Chinese medical experiments is to learn the potential human effects of exposure to powerful EMP and high-powered microwave radiation. One has to wonder whether the medical research also appeared useful for China's military in making sure that their newly developed EMP arsenal designed for use against Taiwan and any targeted U.S. aircraft carrier, would not push the U.S. across the nuclear-response threshold.

Also, China's HEMP capability could be used as a bluff, intended to dissuade the United States from defending Taiwan with U.S. Naval forces. Experts argue the bluff scenario would include China's announcement of a resumption of atmospheric nuclear testing, warn of tests during a specified period, and then attacking Taiwan's infrastructure with conventional forces. China, would then the U.S. response; e.g., whether the U.S. carriers were deployed to defend Taiwan.

China's Super-EMP

Military strategists have long predicted that the first attack in China's Assassin's Mace arsenal would be a Super-EMP. Newly declassified defense intelligence reports reveals that it is already in production. "There is also evidence that China is developing, or has already developed, super-EMP nuclear weapons that generate extraordinarily powerful EMP fields, based partly on design information stolen from the United States," says Dr. Peter Pry, president of the group, EMPact America.

Super-EMP nuclear weapons can exceed the 50,000-volt limit associated with an E1 blast by the nearly instantaneous release of a burst of much higher gamma radiation levels than are known to be produced by these new second-generation nuclear weapons. According to Dr. Pry, Super-EMP weapons can destroy even the best protected U.S. military and civilian electronic systems.

China moves to protect its critical infrastructure

Though the U. S. government has been slow to protect America's electrical grid from a potentially catastrophic electromagnetic event, it appears the Chinese are working to guard their own. Recently, the People's Liberation Army, the PLA, conducted a drill designed to determine how the PLA will respond in the event of an EMP attack on China. Right now, the most likely suspect would be the United States, in the eyes of the PLA, since Beijing and Moscow seem to be getting even more closely intertwined economically as well as militarily.

These drills, which the Chinese military describes as the largest in their history, have already disrupted flights at major Chinese airports. For example, one of the exercises was a simulated EMP attack targeting communications and radar systems. In the simulated attacks, the PLA training exercise included *heavy airstrikes, including electronic disturbance teams, and chemical weapons drills*, per the Chinese state run media.

Col. Chen Hong, a former professor at the PLA Air Force College, told The Daily Telegraph that the deployments were unprecedented.

"The exercises show that our nation has the ability to defend ourselves against any invasion," Col. Chen said. "They are a deterrent to countries around us."

Because of simulated air assaults, these drills significantly affected flights at Chinese airports near the country's east coast. The naval portion of the training involved China's East, North, and South fleets. Also, all airborne and ground missile units of the PLA Air Force were deployed. It was a massive show of strength and intended to send a clear message to the West. China's preparations could have a deterrent effect on any U.S. attempt to take out communications and air-defense systems with the Pentagon's arsenal of electromagnetic weapons.

It is apparent from the comments of Chinese officials that the PLA is attempting to develop a counter to such a capability. Success in having such a counter-measure would cripple the surprise capability that U.S. strike aircraft have employed in the past in Iraq, and potentially against communications and missile defenses of a country; such as Iran or China.

To Washington's credit, it has incorporated the use of EMP weaponry in its arsenal of offensive weapons, and it has taken steps to harden electronics to protect military technologies. However, Washington has been inexplicably negligent in protecting our electrical grid system or the life-staining critical infrastructures that we rely on.

Shouldn't it be a red flag to Washington that China is going through extraordinary steps to protect its critical infrastructure from an EMP attack? Perhaps our lawmakers should take notice that the thing China fears most about other nations is what other nations should fear most about China.

RUSSIA

Russia Strengthens its Nuclear Forces

Like China, Russia is taking significant steps to protect itself from EMP attacks and to enhance both its first-strike and nuclear response capabilities. In 2015, President Vladimir Putin ordered Defense Chiefs to strengthen Russia's strategic nuclear forces, amid rising tensions with the U.S. over the global balance of power.

"New weapons should go to all parts of the nuclear triad of air, sea, and land forces," Putin told his Defense Ministry. He also announced that *action must be taken to improve the effectiveness of missile-attack warning systems and aerospace defense.*

Russia's military will have five new nuclear regiments, equipped with modern missile complexes, by the end of 2016, Defense Minister Sergei Shoigu announced during the same meeting. It is believed that more than ninety percent of the Russia's nuclear forces maintain a permanent state of readiness.

Putin's moves to reinforce Russian nuclear capabilities are reviving Cold War tensions with the U.S. and its allies in the North Atlantic Treaty Organization. Washington warned in June of 2015, that the Kremlin's *nuclear saber-rattling* is undermining stability in an attempt to intimidate European neighbors. Russia's nuclear arsenal, its annexation of Crimea in 2014, and support for separatists in eastern Ukraine, prompted Marine General Joseph Dunford, Chairman of the Joint Chiefs of Staff, to call Russia the most pressing threat to U.S. national security.

Putin, in what appeared to be a statement in preparation for a large-scale conflict, said Russia's military must continue its program of training drills and devote particular attention to the transport of troops over long distances. He further impressed upon his military to prepare their strategic nuclear deterrence and mobility by preparing to airlift anti-aircraft, missile, and electronic forces.

Russia readies for a large-scale regional conflict

Russia has always been considered a war-like nation. Today, about half of Russian nuclear weapons are new, including modern missiles, upgraded aircraft, and a strengthened submarine capacity. Russia has also expanded its military's combat capabilities by reinforcing its western and south-western army groups, and building four bases in the Arctic region.

In response, NATO's troop presence in the Baltic States and central Europe increased sharply in 2015. The U.S. has increased its presence to over two hundred nuclear weapons, situated in Belgium, Italy, the Netherlands, Germany, and Turkey.

Amid a conflict with NATO member Turkey over the shooting down of a Russian warplane near the Syrian border in late 2015, Putin reacted angrily, ordering defense officials to respond harshly to any threats against Russia's forces operating in Syria. Any future threats should face "immediate extermination," he said.

Putin openly claimed that the Russian air campaign in Syria against ISIS and other militants is aimed at protecting Russia from terrorism. In addition, a significant number of airstrikes are being coordinated with both President Bashar al-Assad's forces, and those of the opposition Free Syrian Army, which has more than five thousand troops fighting terrorists with weapons supplied by Russia, Putin stated.

Russia new Doomsday Command Center – the Ilyushin Il-80 Aircraft

Russia's Ministry of Defense has successfully placed into operation its *doomsday flying command center* aboard the Ilyushin Il-80 aircraft. In the case of a full-blown nuclear war, the center is capable of controlling the country's armed forces and to perform necessary offensive or defensive measures. Russia and the U.S. are the only two nations that have developed a command center of this type.

Russia's new airborne command center is primarily designed to have high survivability and reliability in case of a nuclear war. The Ilyushin Il-80's technical capabilities include managing communication networks of Russia's land forces, navy, air, and space forces, as well as their Strategic Missile Forces.

The Ilyushin Il-80 aircraft is meant to be used as an airborne command center for Russian officials, especially President Vladimir Putin, in the event of nuclear war. According to analysts, the aircraft has no external windows, effectively shielding it from a nuclear blast or a high-altitude nuclear electromagnetic pulse. There is only one exterior door, instead of three, and it has a baffle blocking the aft cockpit window, to prevent EMP or RF pulse intrusions during a nuclear attack.

The second-generation command center aboard the aircraft is capable of being operational even when ground-based infrastructure and ground-based command centers have been destroyed. In essence, the Russian Defense Ministry has a fully functional, aerial strategic command post. Ironically, the announcement by the Russian Ministry of Defense came one day after Democrat Congresswoman Tulsi Gabbard, from Hawaii, warned President Barack Obama of an impending nuclear war with Russia.

Russia's anti-satellite missile development – Space Wars?

Russia carried out the first successful flight test of a new anti-satellite missile in 2015, marking a new phase in the global militarization of space. The flight test of Russia's direct ascent, anti-satellite missile, known as *Nudol*, was successful following three prior failures, according to defense officials who were familiar with reports of the test. With the successful anti-satellite missile test, Russia has joined China in arming its forces with strategic space warfare weaponry. Twenty days earlier, China had conducted a flight test of its anti-satellite missile—the *Dong Neng-3*, another direct ascent missile.

Following these reports, a Pentagon spokesman indicated that both Russia and China are developing space warfare capabilities that could threaten critical U.S. satellites. Little information is available on the secretive Russian program. However, like China's recent technological advancements, the Russian direct ascent missile appears to be linked to its missile defense programs.

According to the Russian state-run press, *Novosti*, reports have identified the mobile transporter-launcher for what is described as, "a new Russian long-range missile defense and space defense intercept complex." In response, U.S. General John E. Hyten, the Space Command commander, said he does not want to see conflict extend to space, but also noted we have to be able to defend ourselves. Hyten stated that several nations, including Russia, North Korea, China, and Iran are developing anti-satellite capabilities.

Analysts agree that the space threat to satellites highlights a strategic vulnerability. With as few as two dozen anti-satellite missiles containing EMP warheads, Russia or China could cripple U.S. intelligence, navigation, and communications capabilities that are critical for both military operations and civilian infrastructure.

As Washington cuts our defense budget, the Russians continue to develop their technological abilities to weaponize space and to take out our nation's technology advantage. One Congressman responded to the report, saying, "We can foolishly turn a blind eye to these developments, or acknowledge this threat and develop our capabilities to ensure that our satellites—military and commercial—are not susceptible to attack or blackmail."

China has conducted several tests of anti-satellite weapons, including a 2007 test that left tens of thousands of pieces of dangerous debris floating in space. The *space junk* continues to threaten both manned and unmanned satellites. In 2015, a polar-orbiting National Oceanic and Atmospheric Administration satellite, NOAA 16, mysteriously broke up in space, according to the Air Force's Joint Space Operations Center. An Air Force Space

Command spokesman said no satellites or other objects were detected near the NOAA 16 before its disintegration.

NORTH KOREA

Other nations may not be that far behind Russia and China in the development of EMP weaponry. North Korea has acquired the technology to build an EMP warhead, quite possibly from the Iranians or the Chinese. North Korea routinely test launches satellites that could evade US early warning radars. If these satellites had the ability to launch a nuclear warhead, they would be at the optimal altitude needed to generate a devastating electromagnetic pulse across the entire continental U.S.

North Korea has demonstrated a Fractional Orbital Bombardment System or FOBS capability. FOBS was developed by the Soviet Union in the late sixties to attack the U.S. from over the South Pole, in contrast to their ICBMs that were designed to be launched over the North Pole. Sources within DHS find that North Korea could use its Unha-3 space launch vehicle to deliver a nuclear warhead from a satellite flying over the South Pole.

A HEMP attack on the U.S. would not have to originate from North Korea but could be a missile, such as the SA-2, launched from a freighter off the Eastern Seaboard, or our Gulf Coast. The U.S. has limited missile defense capabilities in these areas of the country. The mutually assured destruction doctrine may not necessarily apply, simply because a missile launched from a freighter could be difficult to identify.

The U.S. anti-missile nuclear defense system that was established to defend against a North Korean missile attack, is plagued with serious technical flaws in the anti-missile interceptors in the U.S. defense system that make it inadequate, according to analysts. Furthermore, even if the technical problems were resolved, a North Korean satellite could potentially come over the undefended South Pole and detonate a HEMP, causing an electromagnetic pulse event for which the U.S. would be virtually defenseless.

Even before the recent revelation that there are defects in the interceptors, experts have warned the U.S. that the anti-ballistic missile system is inadequate because of the limited number of defense systems positioned to intercept an attack from our southern coast. Anti-missile defense systems on the East Coast similarly remain inadequate, with virtually no missile sites located in the southern United States.

In early January of 2016, North Korea claimed that it had successfully tested a *miniaturized* hydrogen bomb.

The announcement was made by a state-controlled television anchor who read a statement calling the test a *perfect success*. Reports from North Korea claimed the testing elevated the country's *nuclear might to the next level* and provided it with a weapon to defend itself against the United States and other enemies.

However, Andrei Lankov, a North Korea expert based in Seoul, South Korea, was *seriously skeptical* that Pyongyang had tested a hydrogen bomb. According to Lankov, North Korea would have needed to divert a large amount of scarce funds to construct such a device, saying it would have been *mission overkill*.

"I believe it did not have the 'signature' of a Hydrogen bomb," said Lankov, who added that he had "absolutely no doubt" that the blast was an atomic test, the fourth carried out since 2006 in defiance of international and United Nations sanctions.

Further, South Korean lawmaker Lee Cheol Woo, told the Associated Press that the country's National Intelligence Service had expressed, in a private briefing, that they believed North Korea had tested an atomic bomb, not a hydrogen bomb.

According to Woo, South Korean intelligence officials said that an estimated explosive yield of six kilotons and a magnitude-4.8 earthquake was detected on the day in question. A smaller blast than the estimated explosive yield of 7.9 kilotons and magnitude-4.9 quake that was reported after a February 2013 nuclear test by North Korea, and only a fraction of a typical successful hydrogen bomb test's explosive yield of hundreds of kilotons. A hydrogen bomb detonation typically yields tens of kilotons.

The U.K. also reacted with outrage. "If a nuclear device has been detonated by North Korea, this is a grave breach of UN Security

Council resolutions and a provocation which I condemn without reservation," British Foreign Secretary Philip Hammond said in a statement. "It underlines the very real threat that North Korea represents to regional and international security."

North Korea goes to great lengths to conceal its tests by conducting them underground and tightly sealing off tunnels or any other vents though which radioactive residue and blast-related noble gases could escape into the atmosphere. The U.S. Air Force has aircraft designed to detect the evidence of a nuclear test, and such aircraft could be deployed from a U.S. base on the Japanese island of Okinawa to search for clues. Japanese media said Tokyo has also mobilized its own reconnaissance aircraft for sorties over the Sea of Japan to try to collect atmospheric data.

In Washington, State Department spokesman John Kirby warned, "we condemn any violation of U.N. Security Council Resolutions and again call on North Korea to abide by its international obligations and commitments," later adding, "we have consistently made clear, that we will not accept [North Korea] as a nuclear state."

Washington and nuclear experts have been skeptical about past North Korean claims to Hydrogen bombs, which are more powerful, and significantly more difficult to make than atomic bombs. North Korea's fourth nuclear explosion will likely push Pyongyang's scientists and engineers closer to their goal of building a high-altitude EMP bomb small enough to place on a missile that can reach the U.S. mainland.

A successful hydrogen bomb test would be a big new step for North Korea. Fusion is the main principle behind the hydrogen bomb, which can be hundreds of times more powerful than atomic bombs that use fission. In a hydrogen bomb, radiation from a nuclear fission explosion sets off a fusion reaction that is responsible for a powerful blast and radioactivity.

Prior to this test, analysts said North Korea hadn't achieved the technology needed to manufacture a miniaturized warhead that could fit on a long-range missile capable of hitting the U.S. mainland. But there is a growing debate on just how far North Korea has advanced in its secretive nuclear and missile programs. Analysts uniformly agree that a missile could be launched from the Gulf of Mexico or via one of North Korea's orbiting satellites.

In late 2015, Kim Jong Un said that his country was, "ready to detonate a self-reliant A-bomb and H-bomb to reliably defend its sovereignty and the dignity of the nation." The comments were met with skepticism by North Korea watchers, who said it was unlikely that Pyongyang possessed the technology to develop such a weapon. These skeptics appear to be convinced.

But nuclear expert, Jeffrey Lewis, wrote on the North Korea-focused 38 North website, "The North has now had a nuclear weapons program for more than 20 years. This program has yielded three nuclear tests. North Korean nuclear scientists have access to their counterparts in Pakistan, possibly Iran and maybe a few other places. We should not expect that they will test the same fission device over and over again."

North Korea's previous nuclear test was in early 2013, and Kim Jong Un did not mention nuclear weapons in his annual New Year's speech. Some outside analysts speculated the dictator was worried about deteriorating ties with China, North Korea's last major ally, which has shown greater frustration at provocations and a possible willingness to allow stronger U.N. sanctions.

IRAN

In early 2015, Iranian President Hassan Rouhani endorsed the use of a nuclear EMP attack against the United States. This revelation came just months before the Obama Administration moved to lift restrictions on the Iranian nuclear program. Clearly, Iran could threaten the existence of the United States by initiating an electromagnetic pulse (EMP) attack using a single nuclear weapon. A nuclear Iran could destroy the most powerful nation on Earth.

Death to America is more than merely an Iranian chant — Tehran's military, has sought the capability to initiate a nuclear EMP attack for years.

In the summer of 2015, at the annual meeting of the Electric Infrastructure Security Summit in Washington, Congressman Trent

Franks quoted from an Iranian military textbook titled *Passive Defense*. In it, the impact of a high altitude nuclear EMP is described in detail. It advocates the use of an EMP attack to defeat an adversary.

The official Iranian military textbook promotes the next generation of warfare that combines coordinated attacks by nuclear and non-nuclear EMP weapons, including cyber warfare. Their stated objective is to destroy electric grids, and collapse entire nations. Iranian military doctrine makes no distinction between nuclear EMP weapons, non-nuclear radio-frequency weapons, and cyber-operations, although it regards nuclear EMP attacks as the ultimate cyber-weapon. In *Passive Defense*, the Iranians advocate EMP as most effective at disabling critical infrastructures without directly causing damage to human life. It provides, in part:

"As a result of not having the other destructive effects that nuclear weapons possess, among them the loss of human life, weapons derived from electromagnetic pulses have attracted attention with regard to their use in future wars. The superficiality of secondary damage sustained, as well as the avoidance of human casualties, serves as a motivation to transform this technology into an advanced and useful weapon in modern warfare."

Because EMP destroys electronics directly, but people indirectly, it is regarded by some as an acceptable use of a nuclear weapon under Sharia Law. *Passive Defense* and other Iranian military treatises seem to ignore the fact that a high-altitude nuclear EMP attack will result in an incredible loss of human life due to the accompanying societal and economic collapse. One Iranian scholar wrote:

"If the world's industrial countries fail to devise effective ways to defend themselves against dangerous electronic assaults, then they will disintegrate within a few years. American soldiers would not be able to find food to eat, nor would they be able to fire a single shot."

The Iranians have done more than just think about an EMP attack.

The Congressional EMP Commission, summarized in Exhibit C, found that Iran has practiced launching missiles and fusing warheads for a HEMP attack, including off a freighter. Iran has apparently practiced surprise EMP attacks utilizing orbiting satellites on south polar trajectories to evade U.S. radars and missile defenses, at altitudes consistent with generating an EMP field covering the continental U.S. Iran launched its fourth satellite on such a path as recently as February 2015.

Through an interpretation of *Passive Defense*, and other Iranian documents, it is clear the Iranians are unconcerned with the deterrent effect of the Mutually Assured Destruction doctrine. They recognize that a single nuclear weapon would complete the list of requirements. Further, because a properly planned, nuclear EMP attack can be conducted by surprise and with anonymity — deterrence may not work against EMP. Deterrence depends on knowing who attacked, and possessing the ability to retaliate. Unlike a nuclear weapon used to blast a city, a high-altitude EMP leaves no collectible bomb debris for forensic analysis to identify the aggressor.

An EMP attack by missile or balloon launched off a freighter could be from many possible actors. Even Yemen's Houthis have Scud missiles, and know how to use them, having recently killed the Chief of Saudi Arabia's air force with a Scud strike on King Khalid Air Force Base.

Hundreds of satellites are in low earth orbit, unseen when approaching the U.S. from the south, which could help disguise the origins of an EMP attack. Also, the EMP could damage not only the means necessary to identify the attacker, but U.S. retaliatory capabilities.

Ayatollah warned that the U.S. deserved a punch in the mouth

One Iranian nuclear weapon is one too many for an Iran ruled by theocratic totalitarian, genocidal imperialists. The spiritual leader of Iran, Ayatollah Ali Khamenei, has warned the U.S. to stay out of his country's affairs and in particular, its nuclear program, which has resumed in late 2015. Speaking on a tour of southeast Iran, Khamenei commented that the US *deserved a punch in the mouth*. Khamenei offered up some additional, more specific harsh words to America. "America is evil and rude. They need to be punched in the mouth," stated Ali Khamenei. "By punched in the mouth, I mean that we need to continue to enrich uranium, build nuclear weapons, get them in the hands of as many terrorists as we can and assist them in detonating them in the northeastern United States."

In response, as Iranians celebrate Ashura, a bloodied Shia Muslim rite, chants of *We shall give our blood for you, Oh Khamenei,* were heard.

Khamenei said that it was not up to the U.S. to decide which countries needed nuclear technology. There is increasing concern within Congress over Iran's missile program, which has been determined by a commission of U.S. scientists, to pose a serious threat to U.S. security.

ISIS, ISIL, Islamic State of DAESH

Let's address what to call this terrorist group first.

ISIS: The militant group, which began as the Iraqi branch of al Qaeda during the U.S. occupation of Iraq, gained this name after it invaded Syria in 2013. ISIS is short for "Islamic State in Iraq and Syria," or "Islamic State of Iraq and al-Sham," which is an old Arabic term for the area.

ISIL: ISIL translates to "the Islamic State of Iraq and the Levant." *The Levant* is a geographical term that refers to the eastern shore of the Mediterranean -- Syria, Lebanon, Palestine, Israel and Jordan. It's the term that the U.S. government uses, stating, "Levant" is a better translation for al-Sham, the Arabic name for the region. But it is also true that *The Levant,* includes the land bridge between Turkey to the north and Egypt to the south. By Arabic tradition and definition, *The Levant* includes Israel. Some scholars, therefore argue that by referring to this terrorist group as ISIL, one is acknowledging that the Nation of Israel does not exist.

Islamic State: This is the English version of what the terror group calls itself. It also claims to be a *caliphate*, which is a state ruled by a *caliph*—Arabic for *successor,*, meaning *successor* to the Islamic Prophet Muhammad. The last acknowledged Muslim caliphate was the Ottoman Empire, which ended in 1923. Many governments and media refuse to use this name because it gives the group legitimacy as a state and a representative of Islam.

Daesh: This is a term the militant group hates. French President François Hollande has used it after Paris attacks in 2015. It's an Arabic acronym for, "al-Dawla al-Islamiya fi al-Iraq wa al-Sham." It can sometimes be spelled DAIISH, Da'esh, or Daech, a popular French version. The hacktivist group, Anonymous, and President Barack Obama have used the term since the deadly terrorist attacks in Paris. ISIS threatened "to cut out the tongue of anyone who publicly used the acronym Daesh, instead of referring to the group by its full name," the Associated Press wrote in September 2014.

By whatever name you choose, ISIS has more than sixty thousand terrorists and is expanding its influence in Syria and Iraq. It's estimated net worth is three billion dollars, generated by nearly two million dollars a day in revenues from black market oil sales and human trafficking. ISIS terrorists pose an *imminent* threat to the U.S. electric grid with the capacity to coordinate a devastating assault on our nation's infrastructure, warned a leading homeland security and terrorism expert.

In a 2015 radio interview, Dr. Pry, outlining the threat, recalled a leaked FERC report that divulged that a coordinated terrorist attack on just nine of the nation's fifty-five thousand electrical power substations could provoke coast-to-coast blackouts for up to eighteen months. Such an attack would mirror the devastating impact of an EMP attack without the need for any nuclear device or delivery system.

Pry pointed specifically to the possibility of ISIS hiring Mexican extremists, such as the Knights Templar drug cartel, which successfully utilized guns and Molotov cocktails to attack numerous Mexican power stations, leaving 11 towns without electricity. Pry surmised that such an attack on the U.S. power grid would not be difficult for the cartel.

"There are ... open-source computer models where you can figure out which of those nine critical transformer substations, if attacked, would take down the whole national power grid," Dr. Pry said. "So something like that could be arranged. It could happen tomorrow. It could happen next week."

Pry also pointed out that in the summer of 2015, al-Qaida attacked power lines in Yemen that left the entire nation without electricity for a day.

ISIS use of Radio Frequency Weapons

Non-nuclear weapons, such as radio frequency weapons, can also generate an EMP, although they are more limited in range than a nuclear weapon. The RFW is capable of causing damage to electronics, and could cause the collapse of critical infrastructures locally, perhaps with cascading effects on larger areas like a major city.

ISIS owns no air force and displays little in the way of air defense weapons. However, experts reveal the terrorist group is trying to close the gap with detailed instructions on social media instructing how to make a homemade weapon that could disable jet fighters. In late 2015, an article was translated by the Middle East Media Research Institute, which tracks jihadist websites, social media, and publications. This instructional guide was produced by the Islamic State's al-Wafa media company and posted on its Telegram and Twitter accounts.

ISIS suggests its fighters target an aircraft's antenna system using an electromagnetic beam, via a satellite link. This beam would, in theory, disrupt the plane's complex set of avionics, potentially making it uncontrollable. The article shows photographs of how to assemble a Radio Frequency Weapon using parts readily available online or in electronics stores. A coordinated attack, combining the use of RFWs by ISIS terrorists or their sympathizers within the United States, could cause a cascading effect on our power grid.

PART FIVE
WHO IS RINGING THE CLARION BELL?

COMMISSION TO ASSESS THE THREAT TO THE UNITED STATES FROM ELECTROMAGNETIC PULSE (EMP) ATTACK

CHAPTER TEN
RESPECTED ADVOCATES

Former Speaker of the House Newt Gingrich

Newt Gingrich is well-known as the architect of the "Contract with America" that led the Republican Party to victory in 1994 by capturing the majority in the U.S. House of Representatives for the first time in forty years. After he was elected Speaker, he disrupted the status quo by moving power out of Washington and back to the American people. Under his leadership, Congress passed welfare reform, the first balanced budget in a generation, and the first tax cut in sixteen years. In addition, the Congress restored funding to strengthen defense and intelligence capabilities, an action later lauded by the bipartisan 9/11 Commission.

Speaker Gingrich has warned the world of his worst nightmare: an electromagnetic pulse. "This could be the kind of catastrophe that ends civilization — and that's not an exaggeration," Gingrich recently said, addressing members of the Electromagnetic Pulse Caucus. The prevailing theory of Speaker Gingrich is that a Russian-made medium-range nuke in the hands of terrorists out on a barge or freighter off the eastern seaboard or in the Gulf of Mexico could do this sort of damage.

Congressman Trent Franks

Congressman Trent Franks is a conservative, Reagan Republican, and is currently serving his seventh term in the United States Congress. Congressman Franks serves on the House Judiciary Committee and is a member of the House Armed Services Committee, serving as the Vice-Chair of the Subcommittee on

Emerging Threats and Capabilities and a member of the Strategic Forces subcommittee.

In his capacity as co-chair of both the Missile Defense and the Electromagnetic Pulse Caucuses, he leads efforts to reduce national security vulnerabilities in our electric energy grids and to increase America's missile defense capability against all enemy missile threats including those potentially launched by jihadists seeking to bring nuclear terrorism to America. Congressman Franks firmly believes the foremost responsibility of our federal government is to provide for our nation's common defense.

Former Congressman Roscoe Bartlett

Former Congressman Roscoe Bartlett was a U.S. Representative from Maryland's 6th congressional district, serving from 1993 to 2013. He is a member of the Republican Party and was a member of the Tea Party Caucus. At the end of his tenure in Congress, Bartlett was the second-oldest serving member of the House of Representatives.

In 1995 Bartlett, who is a scientist, engineer, and inventor with 20 patents, was one of the few members of Congress who understood the threat from EMPs. Between 1995 and 1999, Bartlett held a series of congressional hearings on the EMP threat, including the first unclassified hearings ever held on this subject. The hearings proved that in the wake of the collapse of the Soviet Union, America's defense and intelligence communities stopped paying attention to EMP threats.

In the late '90s, during the U.S.-backed and NATO-led bombing campaign of Serbia, Russians leaders who were backing Serbia, threw an EMP threat in the face of the U.S. congressional delegation. Vladimir Lukin, the former ambassador to the United States, warned that if Russia wanted to hurt the U.S. in retaliation for NATO's bombing of Yugoslavia, Russia could fire a submarine-launched ballistic missile, and detonate a single nuclear warhead at high altitude over the Midwest. He added that if one missile wouldn't do the job, the Russians had more on hand.

Bartlett warned Congress that the resulting electromagnetic pulse would massively disrupt communications and computer systems, effectively shutting down the U.S economy. After hearing this EMP threat, then Congressman Bartlett introduced a bill signed into law by President George W. Bush that established the Congressional EMP Commission in 2001. When the Democrats gained control of Congress in 2006, they re-authorized the EMP Commission that continued its work until 2008. The Congressional EMP Commission report, an Executive Summary of which is found in Exhibit C, warned that terrorists, rogue states, and nations like China and Russia could make a catastrophic EMP attack on the United States.

James Woolsey, Former Director of the Central Intelligence

Mr. Woolsey previously served in the U.S. Government on five different occasions, where he held Presidential appointments in two Republican and two Democratic administrations—most recently (1993-95) as Director of Central Intelligence. During his 12 years of government service, in addition to heading the CIA and the Intelligence Community, Mr. Woolsey was: Ambassador to the Negotiation on Conventional Armed Forces in Europe (CFE), Vienna, 1989–1991; Under Secretary of the Navy, 1977–1979; and General Counsel to the U.S. Senate Committee on Armed Services, 1970–1973. He was also appointed by the President to serve on a part-time basis in Geneva, Switzerland, 1983–1986, as Delegate at Large to the U.S.–Soviet Strategic Arms Reduction Talks (START) and Nuclear and Space Arms Talks (NST). As an officer in the U.S. Army, he was an adviser on the U.S. Delegation to the Strategic Arms Limitation Talks (SALT I), Helsinki and Vienna, 1969–1970.

Mr. Woolsey currently chairs the Strategic Advisory Group of the Washington, D.C. private equity fund, Paladin Capital Group, chairs the Advisory Board of the Opportunities Development Group, and he is Of Counsel to the Washington, D.C. office of the Boston-based law firm, Goodwin Procter. In the above capacities, he specializes in a range of alternative energy and security issues, focusing on the threat we face as a nation from an EMP.

Dr. Peter Vincent Pry

Perhaps there is no greater advocate of protecting our nation from the devastating impact of an EMP, than Dr. Peter Vincent Pry.

From the Task Force on National and Homeland Security website:

"Dr. Pry is Executive Director of the Task Force on National and Homeland Security and Director of the U.S. Nuclear Strategy Forum, both Congressional Advisory Boards, and served on the Congressional EMP Commission, the Congressional Strategic Posture Commission, the House Armed Services Committee, and the CIA.

The Task Force on National and Homeland Security is a privately-funded and operated body with a mandate to educate and help protect the United States from the existential threat posed by a natural or manmade electromagnetic pulse (EMP) catastrophe and other threats vital to U.S. national and homeland security that imperil the survival of the American people. A natural EMP from a great geomagnetic storm, a rare but inevitable threat that many scientists fear is overdue and may soon recur, perhaps as soon as the next solar maximum, could collapse electric grids worldwide and all the critical infrastructures – communications, transportation, banking and finance, food and water – that sustain modern civilization and the lives of millions. A nuclear EMP attack would inflict a similar catastrophe upon the U.S., slowly killing about two-thirds of the national population, 200 million Americans or more dead within one year, from starvation, disease, and societal collapse. Dr. Pry believes such an attack could be executed by both state and non-state actors, in the latter case through the launch of a nuclear-capable ballistic missile from a freighter or other platform off the coast of our country."

Frank Gaffney, Center for Security Policy

From the Center for Security Policy website:

"Frank Gaffney formerly acted as the Assistant Secretary of Defense for International Security Policy during the Reagan

Administration, following four years of service as the Deputy Assistant Secretary of Defense for Nuclear Forces and Arms Control Policy. Previously, he was a professional staff member on the Senate Armed Services Committee under the chairmanship of the late Senator John Tower, and a national security legislative aide to the late Senator Henry M. Jackson.

For twenty-five years, the Center for Security Policy has pioneered the organization, management and direction of public policy coalitions to promote U.S. national security. Even more importantly, the Center's mission has been to secure the adoption of the products of such efforts by skillfully enlisting support from executive branch officials, key legislators, other public policy organizations, opinion-shapers in the media and the public at large.

The philosophy of "Peace through Strength" is not a slogan for military might but a belief that America's national power must be preserved and properly used for it holds a unique global role in maintaining peace and stability.

The process the Center has repeatedly demonstrated is the unique ability that makes the Center the "Special Forces in the War of Ideas": forging teams to get things done that would otherwise be impossible for a small and relatively low-budget organization. In this way, we are able to offer maximum "bang for the buck" for the donors who make our work possible. This approach has enabled the Center to have an outsized impact."

F. Michael Maloof, Author, and former senior security policy analyst to the Secretary of Defense

F. Michael Maloof, a former senior security policy analyst in the Office of the Secretary of Defense, has almost 30 years of federal service in the U.S. Defense Department and as a specialized trainer for border guards and Special Forces in select countries of the Caucasus and Central Asia.

While with the Department of Defense, Maloof was the Director of Technology Security Operations as head of a 10-person team involved in halting the diversion of militarily critical technologies to countries of national security and proliferation concern and those involved in sponsoring terrorism. His office was the liaison to the intelligence and enforcement community within the Office of the Secretary of Defense in halting diversions and using cases that developed from them as early warnings to decision-makers of potential policy issues.

Following the September 11, 2001, terrorist attack on the United States, Maloof was detailed back to report directly to the Under Secretary of Defense for Policy to prepare an analysis of worldwide terrorist networks, determine their linkages worldwide and their relationship to state sponsors. Before his career at the Defense Department, Maloof was a legislative assistant to various U.S. Senators specializing in national security and international affairs.

George Noory, media icon and advocate of EMP preparedness

George Noory, the host of the nationally syndicated program, Coast to Coast AM, says if he weren't a national radio talk show host, he'd be in politics. Heard by millions of listeners, Coast To Coast AM airs on I Heart Radio, SiriusXM Satellite, and over six hundred radio stations worldwide.

In 2014, Noory announced a campaign to protect and insulate the U.S. power grid against an EMP event or attack via nuclear weapons, ballistic missiles, and solar flares, all of which could endanger the lives of millions of Americans. The threat of an electromagnetic pulse event or attack on the U.S. has prompted Noory, host of "Coast to Coast AM," the most-listened-to overnight radio program in North America, to launch a campaign to prepare a defense.

"I implore all individual states, the President and members of Congress to immediately develop a plan to protect our power grid," said Noory. "The preservation of our great nation and the lives of its people are critical." The goal is to protect and insulate the U.S. power grid against an EMP event or attack from a solar flare, nuclear weapon or ballistic missile, all of which could endanger the lives of millions of Americans, according to Noory.

CHAPTER ELEVEN
THE EMP COMMISSION

The EMP Commission

Through the warnings of Representatives Franks and Bartlett, Congress finally began to recognize the potential threat of this powerful nuclear phenomenon. Congress established the EMP Commission under the National Defense Authorization Act of 2001 in order to provide an independent assessment of this threat against the United States. The authorizing provision directed that the EMP Commission investigate and report to Congress its findings and recommendations for the United States concerning four aspects of the EMP threat:

The duties of the EMP Commission, among other things, included assessing the following:

1. The nature and magnitude of potential high-altitude EMP threats to the United States from all potentially hostile states or non-state actors that have or could acquire nuclear weapons and ballistic missiles enabling them to perform a high-altitude EMP attack against the United States within the next 15 years

2. The vulnerability of United States military and especially civilian systems to an EMP attack, giving special attention to vulnerability of the civilian infrastructure as a matter of emergency preparedness

3. The capability of the United States to repair and recover from damage inflicted on United States military and civilian systems by an EMP attack

4. The feasibility and cost of hardening select military and civilian systems against EMP attack.

The Commission is charged with identifying any steps it believes should be taken by the United States, to better protect its military and civilian systems from EMP attack.

Multiple reports and briefings associated with this effort were produced by the EMP Commission including the often cited Critical National Infrastructures Report.

According to the Commission report, protecting the United States against the evolving EMP threat will require a mix of active defenses, passive defenses, and policy changes. Specifically, the United States should:

- Develop a clear policy about how it would respond to an EMP attack. An adversary may be emboldened to use EMP because the U.S. has no clear retaliation policy. As the commission's report makes clear, an EMP attack could devastate both civilian and military assets without harming humans--in the short term. An adversary could therefore, calculate that the United States would respond less severely to an EMP strike than it would to a more traditional attack that results in physical destruction and casualties. That makes EMP very attractive. It could carry decreased risk but promise great reward. By itself, a policy guaranteeing significant retaliation may not deter all hostile groups from using EMP, but it may deter some. Better yet, a policy to retaliate combined with other actions--such as installing active defenses, increased passive defenses, and assuring military survivability--would decrease the likelihood of an EMP attack against the United States because such measures would make a strike less likely to succeed. If it did succeed, the consequences for the United States would be minimal. Thus, the value of an EMP strike would be significantly reduced, but the risk of launching an attack would be greatly increased because the U.S. would not only have a policy to retaliate, but also the capability.

- Protect the vital nodes of America's power grid and telecommunications systems. Much of America's power grid and telecommunications systems is vulnerable to EMP attack. In the near term, hardening America's entire critical infrastructure is not feasible. However, protecting those elements of U.S. infrastructure that would be essential to any post-EMP recovery (e.g., large turbines, generators, high-voltage transformers, and electronic telecommunications switching systems) is possible. These major nodes are not only critical to the nation's power-grid and telecommunications capability, but would be extremely difficult and timeconsuming to rebuild or repair. Protecting these critical infrastructure nodes may be expensive in the near term, but it could save the nation significantly in both money and lives in the future.

- Conduct a national vulnerability assessment and prepare a national recovery plan. Although protecting the nation's entire electronic and telecommunications systems against EMP strike is unreasonable, protecting some of those assets is possible. The Department of Homeland Security (DHS) should work with the private sector to identify which parts of the nation's power grid and telecommunications infrastructure are critical to preserving the nation's core capabilities. These assets would also be the most essential to recovery efforts in a post-EMP environment. By protecting these nodes, the United States could significantly reduce the time needed to recover from an attack. Additionally, DHS should develop a contingency plan for recovery from an EMP attack that would minimize confusion.

- Retrofit portions of the U.S. armed forces to ensure EMP survivability. The United States' military must end its nearly complete vulnerability to an EMP strike. This glaring hole in U.S. defenses is a liability that America's adversaries will surely exploit if it is not corrected. As with civilian infrastructure, hardening America's entire military apparatus against EMP is prohibitively expensive. However, the nation should invest the resources to retrofit enough of the military's land, sea, and air assets to guarantee any potential adversary that the U.S. will be able to respond comprehensively to any kind of attack. Hardening military equipment against EMP costs approximately 10 percent of the original cost of the equipment. While this is high, it is a necessary expense given the risk.

- Begin building military systems that are engineered with EMP protections. Although retrofitting against EMP is extremely expensive, engineering EMP resistance into a system from the beginning adds only about 1 percent to the system cost. Given that so much of military equipment is already old and that force transformation will result in many new systems and platforms, now is an opportune time to begin dealing with this problem. In addition to saving money by incorporating EMP resistance into new systems instead of retrofitting existing equipment, America's transformed military will increasingly rely on many sophisticated electronic networks and systems. A successful EMP strike against U.S. forces that disrupted or destroyed these systems would effectively turn America's technological advantage into a distinct liability.

- Deploy ballistic missile defense. The surest way to protect the United States from a high-altitude EMP is by deploying a ballistic missile defense system that can intercept and destroy a warhead before it could be detonated above the U.S. This would prevent an EMP attack and eliminate any potential harm to U.S. systems, and it could even deter rogue leaders from considering the use of EMP. Deploying a missile defense architecture that can intercept a missile early in flight (during the ascent phase) would render rogue missiles ineffective, thereby undermining the rationale to use them. Moreover, because protecting America's entire civilian electronic infrastructure is not fiscally feasible and because a ballistic missile is the most likely delivery vehicle for an EMP attack, the most prudent method to protect America is a missile defense system that could destroy a ballistic missile before it reaches U.S. airspace.

As the EMP Commission reported, the threat of an EMP attack on America is real and one for which the United States is vulnerable. While the world focused on weapons of mass destruction and ballistic missiles, the scientists and policy analysts that made up the EMP Commission believed it was imperative that an EMP attack must be considered with equal weight. The profound impact that an EMP attack would have on America—a developed, modern, electronically oriented country, has forced other similarly situated nations to reassess their protection against such attack.

Looking toward the future, America should consider its options for protecting its infrastructure against such a debilitating attack. Those options are limited but include deploying an effective missile defense system and hardening electronic systems against EMP. As the commission indicated, the implications of an EMP attack need to be assessed further with greater severity and inevitability as America considers possible protective actions against this threat.

The EMP Commission was reestablished via the National Defense Authorization Act for Fiscal Year 2016, to continue its efforts to monitor, investigate, make recommendations, and report to Congress on the evolving threat to the United States from a high-altitude electromagnetic pulse attack.

CHAPTER TWELVE
UNITED STATES POLICY STANCE

Protecting the homeland means more than our borders

The Congressional EMP Commission spent eight years developing a plan to protect all infrastructures from EMP – a plan that would also mitigate threats from cyber-attack, sabotage, and natural disasters. The Commission estimated in 2008 it would cost $2 billion to harden the grid's critical nodes (i.e., roughly 2,000 large and medium-sized transformers and their associated SCADA systems, etc.) The remainder of the proposed plan could have been implemented within five years, at a cost of $20 billion.

Those sums are modest when compared with the unimaginably high costs associated with trying to recover from a HEMP attack. To put this in perspective had Washington adopted the Commission's plan, it would have been completed at the time of this book's release. By comparison, $20 billion, the high estimate of the Commission's suggested plan, is equal to seventeen days of interest on our national debt. The cost, however, has been an excuse for inaction.

In 2008, the bipartisan Electromagnetic Pulse Commission testified before Congress that U.S. society is not structured, nor does it have the means, to provide for the needs of three hundred million Americans without electricity.

- The current strategy for recovery from a failure of the electric grid leaves us ill-prepared to respond effectively to a manmade or naturally occurring EMP event that would potentially result in damage to vast numbers of components nearly simultaneously on an unprecedented geographic scale;

- Should the electrical power system be lost for any substantial period, the consequences are likely to be catastrophic to society, including potential casualties of more than ninety percent of the population, according to the Chairman of the EMP Commission;

- Adverse impacts on the electric infrastructure are potentially catastrophic in an EMP event, unless practical steps are taken to provide protection for critical elements of the electric system.

Finally, most experts predict that the occurrence of severe geomagnetic storms is inevitable; it is only a matter of when.

In 2015, the Senate Homeland Security and Governmental Affairs Committee debated a bill to protect our critical infrastructure as the power industry urged lawmakers to keep the complexity of the electric grid in mind as part of the legislation. The bill, introduced by Sen. Ron Johnson, R-Wis., the committee Chairman, called for the federal government to develop a strategy to protect critical infrastructure from geomagnetic disturbances caused by solar storms, and electromagnetic pulses, which are generated by nuclear and non-nuclear devices.

The bill included an amendment by Johnson, acting under lobbyist pressure, which addressed electric cooperative industry concerns. Lobbyists argued that combining electromagnetic pulse and geomagnetic disturbance threats in planning, preparing or mitigating efforts were improper. They suggested pulling the threats apart and addressing them separately.

The current legislation in the House combines the two types of threats. According to industry representatives, they should be treated separately because they require distinctly different planning, preparation, mitigation, and recovery efforts.

The power sector claims it practices *defense in depth* to balance preparation, prevention, response, and recovery for various hazards to electric grid operations. The industry's priorities are to protect the most critical grid components against the most likely threats, build in system resiliency, and to develop contingency plans for response and recovery.

One industry representative, Bridgette Bourge, said, "When considered as part of the broader spectrum of potential threats to the electric grid, a nuclear-induced electromagnetic pulse is considered an extremely low likelihood, high-consequence event. That doesn't mean the electric industry disregards or ignores its significance, but that it is considered appropriately as part of a broader risk management strategy."

"These events, and threats of these events, are very different and should be treated that way," said Bourge. "They are unique in how and what they impact. It is true that a geomagnetic storm is significantly less damaging than a nuclear EMP."

In other words, we don't think there is a likelihood that a high-altitude electromagnetic pulse attack will take place in the U.S., and therefore we don't want to go through the expense of hardening the power grid against it.

CHAPTER THIRTEEN
RECENT LEGISLATIVE HISTORY

U.S. Congress

In 2005, the Final Report of the Congressional Commission on the Strategic Posture of the United States was released and provided in part:

"The United States should take steps to reduce the vulnerability of the nation and the military to attacks with weapons designed to produce electromagnetic pulse (EMP) effects. We make this recommendation although the Commission is divided over how imminent a threat this is. Some commissioners believe it to be a high priority threat, given foreign activities and terrorist intentions.

"Others see it as a serious potential threat, given the high level of vulnerability. Those vulnerabilities are of many kinds. U.S. power projection forces might be subjected to an EMP attack by an enemy calculating – mistakenly – that such an attack would not involve risks of U.S. nuclear retaliation. The homeland might be attacked by terrorists or even state actors with an eye to crippling the U.S. economy and American society. From a technical perspective, it is possible that such attacks could have catastrophic consequences. For example, successful attacks could shut down the electrical system, disable the internet and computers—and the economic activity on which they depend—incapacitate transportation systems (and thus the delivery of food and other goods), etc.

"Prior commissions have investigated U.S. vulnerabilities and found little activity under way to address them. Some limited defensive measures have been ordered by the Department of Defense to give some protection to important operational communications. But EMP/IEMI vulnerabilities have not yet been addressed effectively by the Department of Homeland Security. Doing so could take several years. The Congressional EMP Commission has recommended numerous measures that would mitigate the damage that might be wrought by an EMP attack."

In response to the report, it took the Stimulus Bill of February 2009 to allocate $11 billion to the Department of Energy for "smart grid activities, including modernizing the electric grid. Unless such improvements in the electric grid are focused in part on reducing EMP vulnerabilities, vulnerability might well increase."

GRID ACT 2010 -The Grid Reliability and Infrastructure Defense Act

In 2010, the House passed the GRID Act, which would have protected 300 of the country's biggest transformers. The measure died in the Senate later that year.

In a surprising election-year gambit, Alaska Sen. Lisa Murkowski gutted the legislation despite strong bipartisan support that would have protected the U.S. power grid from solar flares and Electromagnetic Pulse weapons. Her staff claimed she preferred a "clean" energy bill backed by Senate Democrats.

The original bill, known as the GRID Act, authorized the federal government to take emergency measures to protect some 300 giant power transformers around the country. It passed the House of Representatives by a unanimous voice vote in August, an unusual show of bipartisan support in this Congress.

But when it went to the Senate, the bill was gutted of the measures to protect the power grid from EMP attack by Murkowski and committee chairman Jeff Bingamon, D-N.M., while other portions of the bill were added to her energy bill, S. 1462, the American Clean Energy Act of 2009.

"Sen. Murkowski stripped H.R. 5026 of the main elements designed to protect our infrastructure and did not add them to her bill," said Andrea Lafferty, executive director of the Traditional Values Coalition. An aide to Murkowski said that Murkowski voted for stripping out the EMP provisions of the bill on practical, not political, grounds.

"The bill was going nowhere. The administration opposed it, and favored a government-wide effort, not a piecemeal approach." The aide added that blaming Murkowski, the ranking Republican on the Energy Committee, for altering legislation being managed by the majority Democrats was "an election-year gambit by far right wing groups. Murkowski did not place a hold on the House bill."

The SHIELD Act – Secure High-voltage Infrastructure for Electricity from Lethal Damage Act

The SHIELD Act is the first legitimate attempt Congress has taken to protect the power grid from an EMP attack or solar flare. Reps. Trent Franks and Yvette Clarke introduced the bipartisan SHIELD Act, which mandates many of the same safeguards as outlined in the GRID Act of 2010.

Here is what the SHIELD ACT would do:

- The SHIELD Act, which amends section 215 of the Federal Power Act, encourages cooperation between industry and government in the development, promulgation, and implementation of standards and processes that are necessary to address the current shortcomings and vulnerabilities of the electric grid from a major EMP event

- The SHIELD Act incorporates most of the EMP-related language of HR 5026 from the 111th Congress, which passed overwhelmingly through the House, but was stalled in the Senate during the Lame Duck due mostly to additional language regarding cyber-security threats

- The SHIELD Act also requires that standards be developed within six months, as opposed to one year, of enactment, to ensure a faster timeline of protection.

When the bill was introduced, former Speaker Gingrich voiced his support, but the House Energy and Commerce Committee blocked the legislation.

GRID ACT 2014

The Grid Reliability and Infrastructure Defense (GRID) Act would allow the Federal Energy Regulatory Committee—*FERC*— to issue emergency orders to protect the electricity infrastructure from threats, said Rep. Henry Waxman (D-Calif.) and Sen. Ed Markey (D-Mass.), the bill's sponsors. FERC would also attain regulatory power to protect against grid vulnerabilities.

"Unless we act now, the United States will continue to remain vulnerable to the 21st century cyber armies preparing to wage war on our banking, health care, and defense systems by knocking out America's electricity grid," Markey said in a statement. "The GRID Act will help secure our nation's electrical grid against devastating damage from physical or cyber terrorist attacks, and from natural disasters."

Markey previously sponsored the GRID Act in 2010 when he was in the House. It passed there, but not in the Senate.

"We will remain vulnerable to attacks that could cause devastating blackouts until security is increased and regulatory gaps are closed," Waxman said. "The GRID Act provides regulators the authority they need to ensure that the grid is adequately protected."

The bill's provisions, and the rules FERC would be authorized to establish are designed to protect against "physical, cyber, electromagnetic pulse and other threats" to the electric grid.

Electric utilities opposed the GRID Act the last time it was proposed. The National Rural Electric Cooperative Association said the bill would give FERC too much power over utilities.

CRITICAL INFRASTRUCTURE PROTECTION ACT (CIPA) 2015

In the summer of 2015, the House of Representatives approved unanimously H.R. 3410, the Critical Infrastructure Protection Act (CIPA). This legislation marks a breakthrough. For the first time in four years, Congress has acted to begin to protect the nation's most critical of critical infrastructures; the U.S. electrical grid. It now falls to the Senate and to President Obama to ensure that the House-passed bill becomes the law of the land.

CIPA's lead sponsors were Reps. Trent Franks (R-AZ), a senior member of the House Armed Services Committee and co-chairman of the Electromagnetic Pulse (EMP) Caucus, and Pete Sessions (R-TX), the chairman of the powerful House Rules Committee. The measure enjoyed strong bipartisan support, including from the House Homeland Security Committee's Chairman Michael McCaul (R-TX), and the Chairman and Ranking Member of the Committee's Subcommittee on Cybersecurity, Infrastructure Protection, and Security Technologies, Reps. Patrick Meehan (R-PA) and Yvette Clark (D-NY).

The CIPA legislation requires the Department of Homeland Security to:

- Include in national planning scenarios the threat of electromagnetic pulse (EMP) which would entail the education of the owners and operators of critical infrastructure, as well as emergency planners and emergency responders at all levels of government of the threat of EMP events

- Engage in research and development aimed at mitigating the consequences of naturally occurring or man-caused EMP events; and

- Produce a comprehensive plan to protect and prepare the critical infrastructure of the American homeland against EMP events.

TRANSPORTATION BILL AMENDMENT – November 2015

The transportation bill that President Obama signed in November of 2015 includes provisions intended to protect the grid from terrorist attacks and natural disasters, giving the Secretary of Energy emergency powers and creating a Strategic Transformer Reserve.

The legislation, which will provide $305 billion in highway funding over five years, cleared the Senate 83-16, following a 359-65 vote in the House. The bill represents both a vindication and a rebuke of former FERC Chairman Jon Wellinghoff's controversial campaign to raise awareness of the grid's vulnerability to sabotage.

It also checked off an item on current FERC Chairman Norman Bay's wish list. Testifying before the House Energy and Power Subcommittee, Bay said it was essential that the government have emergency powers to respond to both an EMP attack and cyber attack. "That emergency authority does not need to reside with FERC. It could reside elsewhere in the federal government," Bay said. "But someone needs to have it."

Title 55 of the bill includes five "Energy Security" sections, including Section 61003, which authorizes the President to declare a grid security emergency in response to a geomagnetic storm, electromagnetic pulse, or cyber attack. Such a declaration would authorize the Energy Secretary to issue emergency orders to protect or restore electric infrastructure critical to *national security, economic security, public health or safety.*

Section 61004 requires the Secretary to submit a plan to Congress within a year for the development of a Strategic Transformer Reserve, including enough large transformers (100 MVA or higher) and trailer-mounted emergency mobile substations *to temporarily replace critically damaged large power transformers and substations that are critical electric infrastructure or serve defense and military installations.*

These provisions are a response to the April 2013 attack on Pacific Gas and Electric's substation in Metcalf, California. At least two gunmen were believed involved in the attack on the 500/230-kV substation near San Jose, causing more than $15 million in damage that shut down the substation for nearly a month. The gunmen targeted transformer radiators, firing an estimated 150 rounds and hitting 10 of 11 banks. The Metcalf attack was the most significant incident of domestic terrorism involving the grid to date.

Former Chairman Wellinghoff found himself under fire after The Wall Street Journal quoted him in an article about a confidential FERC analysis that concluded the country's entire grid could be shut down for months by disabling only nine critical substations. Transformers are typically custom designed and can take over eighteen months to replace. The WSJ article did not identify the locations of those substations or its source for the study, but it quoted Wellinghoff as saying, "there are probably less than 100 critical high voltage substations on our grid in this country that need to be protected from a physical attack."

NERC, members of Congress and Wellinghoff's former FERC colleagues complained that the disclosures had jeopardized, not improved, security. The Department of Energy Inspector General Gregory Friedman warned that FERC's protection of information on the vulnerability of the grid is "severely lacking" and suggested that Wellinghoff had offered too much information when questioned about the disclosures.

As a result of Wellinghoff's disclosures, Section 61003 requires FERC to develop regulations governing how it classifies information as critical electric infrastructure information (CEII), including "appropriate sanctions for commissioners, officers, employees or agents of the commission who knowingly and willfully disclose critical electric infrastructure information in a manner that is not authorized." The section also exempts CEII from disclosure under federal, state or local public records laws.

In testimony before the House subcommittee, current Commissioner Cheryl LaFleur suggested policymakers have more work to do.

"I think the reliability standards that we've put in place, which require every transmission owner to identify the most critical facilities and protect them, are an important step," she said. "But I think beyond that, a lot of the protection has to come from how we build the grid — building more redundancy so we kind of 'de-criticalize' those places so that a physical attack won't cause as much damage, and building in more standardization. If something goes wrong we can share transformers more, rather than having to build a custom one in every place."

GAO REPORT: CRITICAL INFRASTRUCTURE PROTECTION: Preliminary Observations on DHS Efforts to Address Electromagnetic Threats to the Electric Grid

What the GAO Found

As of July 2015, the Department of Homeland Security (DHS) reported taking several actions that could help address the electromagnetic threats to the electric grid. GAO's preliminary analysis of DHS's actions indicated they fell into four categories: (1) developing reports, (2) identifying mitigation efforts, (3) strategy development and planning, and (4) conducting exercises.

In other words, they did what our government does best—talk about it.

The GAO's Report was of the DHS when it wrote: "Preliminary findings indicate that DHS Actions to Address Electromagnetic Threats were Conducted Independently of the EMP Commission Recommendations." In other words, they did their own thing.

The DHS reported its actions were not taken in response to the 2008 recommendations of the Commission to Assess the Threat to the United States from Electromagnetic Pulse Attack (EMP Commission). The GAO also recognized that DHS does not have a statutory obligation to specifically address the recommendations, but the implementation of them could help mitigate electromagnetic impacts to the electric grid, such as helping to assure the protection of high-value transmission assets. Moreover, the GAO's preliminary work suggested that DHS, in conjunction with the Department of Energy (DOE), has not adequately addressed an essential critical infrastructure protection responsibility—identification of precise internal agency roles and responsibilities related to addressing electromagnetic threats. For example, although DHS recognized one component as the lead for assessing solar weather risks, the component has not yet identified any specific roles related to collecting or analyzing risk information.

DHS has also coordinated with federal and industry stakeholders to address some, but not all risks to the electrical grid, since the EMP Commission issued its recommendations. The GAO preliminarily identified eight projects in which the DHS coordinated efforts to help protect the power grid, including developing plans to address long-term power outages, participation in exercises, and research and development activities. Although these are positive steps, the GAO's preliminary work indicated that the DHS has not effectively coordinated with utilities to identify critical assets or collect necessary risk information, among other responsibilities. The GAO announced it will continue to assess the issues in this statement as it completes its work and will publish a report with the final results in late 2015.

NDAA 2016, Section 1089: EMP Commission revived

Section 1089 of the bill restores the EMP Commission, which previously had a run from 2001 to 2008. Also, the EMP Commission's charter will expand to make clear its charge also covers non-nuclear EMP weapons, EMP-like effects from natural forces, and the study of how potential adversaries might propose to use EMP in their military doctrine.

The Commission was directed to assess the following:

(1) The vulnerability of electric-dependent military systems in the United States to a manmade or natural EMP event, giving special attention to the progress made by the Department of Defense, other Government departments and agencies of the United States, and entities of the private sector in taking steps to protect such systems from such an event

(2) The evolving current and future threat from state and non-state actors of a manmade EMP attack employing nuclear or non-nuclear weapons

(3) New technologies, operational procedures, and contingency planning that can protect electronics and military systems from the effects a manmade or natural EMP event

(4) Among the States, if State grids are protected against manmade or natural EMP, which States should receive highest priority for protecting critical defense assets

(5) The degree to which vulnerabilities of critical infrastructure

systems create cascading vulnerabilities for military systems

STATE LEGISLATION

Policy makers on a local level have already begun to get smart and challenge the electrical industry to higher standards. At the National Council of State Legislatures in 2015, several lawmakers said they're preparing legislation similar to a 2013 bill introduced in Maine. Here are a few of the more significant state legislative actions:

- On June 11, 2013, the State of Maine passed the first legislation in the nation to protect the electric grid against electromagnetic pulse (EMP) and geomagnetic disturbance (GMD). EMPs, such as high-altitude nuclear explosions, and GMDs, such as major solar flares and storms, have the potential to critically disrupt or destroy the electric grid.

- On March 10, 2015, Virginia Governor, Terry McAuliffe signed a bill requiring the commonwealth's Department of Emergency Management (DEM) to plan for responses to disasters caused by electromagnetic pulses (EMPs). This requirement is part of the DEM's overall mission of disaster preparedness.

- Arizona implemented a requirement in 2014 for its emergency management agency to incorporate EMP preparedness into its disaster planning. Louisiana's preparedness office is examining the possible effects of an EMP event. In 2013, Kentucky set up an interagency working group to examine EMP preparedness efforts.

- In Texas, there are currently two bills that address the protection of the electrical grid. Specifically, they relate to a study by the Electric Reliability Council of Texas on securing critical infrastructure from electromagnetic, geomagnetic, terrorist, and cyber attack threats. They are House Bill 2289, and Senate Bill 1398.

The FAST ACT—Fixing America's Surface Transportation Act

There is good news. On December 4, 2015, President Obama signed into law the "FAST Act"—an acronym for Fixing America's Surface Transportation Act. Part of a massive highway and transportation bill, the FAST Act also includes energy security amendments to the Federal Power Act ("FPA"), several of which affect utilities and others in the electric industry. These changes potentially impact owners, operators, and users of electric infrastructure; even relatively small, intrastate utilities not ordinarily subject to control by the Federal Energy Regulatory Commission ("FERC").

The FAST Act creates a new Section 215A in the FPA, much of which revolves around the newly-defined terms *critical electric infrastructure* and critical electric infrastructure information. *Critical electric infrastructure* ("CEI") is broadly defined to include both physical and virtual systems and assets of the bulk-power system, whose destruction or incapacity would have a negative impact on national or economic security, public health, or safety. *Critical electric infrastructure information* ("CEII") could mean potentially any information related to CEI, and generated by or submitted to FERC or any other federal agency, other than classified national security information.

The primary purpose of the act is to encourage information sharing between the public sector and the private sector. The FAST Act reduces the restrictions of disclosures of CEII, and also promotes information sharing among government and industry participants. As suggested in the definition of CEII, the full impact of these provisions will depend on rules FERC must promulgate within the next year, which will determine both procedures and substantive criteria for designating CEII and preventing its unauthorized disclosure. The Act itself does specify, however, that no federal, state, local, or tribal entity is required to disclose CEII on the basis of any public disclosure law at any level, including the federal Freedom of Information Act (FOIA). Our government seems intent on protecting on our grid, and not letting our adversaries know how we're doing it.

Depending on the rules regarding implementation, these provisions could prevent disclosure of a wide swath of industry information submitted to the federal government, including FERC filings. By definition, CEII might include, any "information related to critical electric infrastructure, or proposed critical electrical infrastructure, generated by or provided to [FERC] or other Federal agency, other than classified national security information," and designated according to the rules to be established. Significantly, the new federal protection preempts state and local laws, preventing CEII disclosure even by a state or local agency pursuant to a state or local public disclosure law. However, to be designated as CEII, the information must have been generated by or submitted to a federal agency.

The new Section 215A gives the Department of Energy ("DOE") increased authority in case of a "grid security emergency," including malicious physical or electronic acts, magnetic disturbances due to the sun, direct physical attacks, and related threats and reliability disruptions. When the President identifies such an emergency, DOE can order emergency measures the Secretary of Energy ("Secretary") deems necessary to protect or restore CEI reliability. FAST requires little administrative process prior to issuance of these emergency orders. Though the DOE must adopt procedures for such cases, the Secretary may issue emergency orders "with or without notice, hearing, or report." The President must notify, but does not require the consent of Congress in making the emergency determination. It will be incumbent upon the DOE to consult with affected governments and CEI owners and operators.

An emergency order under the new FPA section 215A could affect "any owner, user, or operator" of CEI in the U.S., even entities not ordinarily subject to FERC jurisdiction (for example, municipally owned utilities, rural electric cooperatives, and federal power marketing agencies like the Tennessee Valley Authority and Bonneville Power Administration). The DOE's new authority also explicitly extends to the North American Electric Reliability Corporation ("NERC") and other regional power suppliers.

To overcome industry objections regarding the costs of implementing the law, if CEI owners, operators, or users incur expenses in complying with an emergency order, but cannot recover those costs through their existing rate structures, the new law directs FERC to establish mechanisms for recovery of those costs.

The issue of backup transformers has finally been addressed. The new law requires DOE's Office of Electricity Delivery and Energy Reliability, in consultation with FERC, NERC, and the Electricity Subsector Coordinating Council, to submit a plan to Congress evaluating the feasibility of establishing a Strategic Transformer Reserve for storage in strategic locations of spare large power transformers and emergency mobile substations. The plan would determine adequate amounts and locations to temporarily replace critically damaged large power transformers and substations. The reserve would reduce the vulnerability of U.S. critical infrastructure to physical or cyber attack, electromagnetic pulse, solar disturbance of the earth's magnetic field, severe weather, and earthquake.

The DOE's plan must include the funding options available to establish and maintain the Strategic Transformer Reserve, including imposing fees on owners and operators of bulk-power system facilities and CEI. Additionally, the plan must assess the possibility of imposing fees on the large power transformer owner/operators and substations that constitute CEI, to pay for Strategic Transformer Reserve operating costs.

Electric cooperatives have been concerned about the conflicts between the state laws and regulations imposed by the federal government. FAST amends Section 202(c) of the FPA (FERC's existing emergency authority) to clarify that FERC emergency orders override federal, state, and local environmental laws. Congress intended to resolve the perceived conflict facing power plant operators, who feared violating either an emergency order from FERC or environmental regulations if an emergency arose.

Consistent with this administration's concern for the environment, any emergency order must still minimize environmental impacts and must be consistent with all applicable environmental laws, "to the maximum extent practicable." FERC must also consult with federal environmental regulators, before an order can remain in effect longer than ninety days. Further, FERC must incorporate any condition submitted by the environmental agency, or explain its determination of why that submitted condition would impede an adequate emergency response.

These specific provisions regarding the environment, ensure that utilities and other operators of electric generation and transmission facilities can now comply with FERC emergency orders with the enhanced assurance that they will not incur environmental liability, whether civil (including citizen suits) or criminal. The exemptions afforded under FAST provides that such acts or omissions, even when taken to "voluntarily comply" with an emergency order, will not be considered violations of any federal, state, or local environmental law. This protection continues, even if courts later alter or strike down the underlying FERC order. The existing language of Section 202(c) does not appear to limit FERC's emergency authority to utilities otherwise under its jurisdiction, so it appears that the new exemption could benefit virtually any operator of electric infrastructure, should an emergency arise.

The FAST Act offers the electric power sector several benefits, most notably, the exemption from environmental regulations to the extent that they conflict with FERC emergency orders, improved cost recovery for compliance with such orders, and also some degree of added protection of sensitive information from public disclosure. On the other hand, system participants will now be subject to broader federal control, especially in emergency situations. The Strategic Transformer Reserve planning also foreshadows potentially significant costs that Congress could impose on owners, operators, and users of generation and grid assets in the future. Conclusively, most of the new agency powers and responsibilities just enacted apply not only to utilities and grid operators accustomed to dealing with FERC, but also to entities not ordinarily subject to FERC jurisdiction.

SUGGESTIONS TO U.S. POLICYMAKERS

At Heritage.org, Senior Policy Analyst, Michaela Dodge and Policy Analyst, Jessica Zuckerman provided this list of what Congress and the Administration should do:

- Mandate additional research into mitigating EMP threats. Similar to what Maine is doing, the U.S. should undertake additional research into how an EMP would affect electronics and electrical systems and how these vulnerabilities can be removed or lessened.

- Determine which countries could undertake EMP attacks. The U.S. should understand where potential EMP attacks could come from and produce intelligence estimates on nations that are pursuing or already have weapons capable of producing an EMP. This information can then be used to better inform policymakers on how best to respond to potential threats and prevent EMP attacks from occurring.

- Improve and fully fund U.S. missile defense. Ballistic missiles are one of the most effective means of delivering an EMP. U.S. missile defense should be advanced to address the threat, especially as the East Coast remains less protected than the West Coast. Improved command-and-control features and interceptors tied to forward-deployed radar would give the Standard Missile-3 (SM-3) interceptor the ability to counter long-range ballistic missiles in the late midcourse stage of flight. The government should improve the SM-3's ability to intercept short-range ballistic missiles in the ascent phase of flight. Ultimately, the U.S. should develop and deploy space-based missile defense, the best way to protect the U.S. and its allies from ballistic missiles.

- Develop a National Recovery Plan and National Planning Scenario for EMP. The catastrophic cost of an EMP event means that it deserves careful preparation and planning. Such plans should take the advice of the EMP commission and employ a risk-based approach that recognizes that certain infrastructure—particularly electrical and telecommunication systems upon which all other sectors depend—is most important in preparing for and recovering from an EMP event. Additionally, DHS should have a National Planning Scenario dedicated to EMP so that local, state, and federal authorities understand what would happen in an EMP event and what their respective responsibilities are in terms of both response and recovery.

- Prepare and protect critical cyber infrastructure. Cyber infrastructure is completely and uniquely dependent on the power grid, which makes it particularly vulnerable to an EMP. The U.S. should explore ways to protect and shield the circuit boards of critical networks. Additionally, the U.S. should consider the interdependency between the nation's cyber infrastructure and the other critical infrastructures and take actions to prevent cascading failures.

Chapter Fourteen
U. S. Department of Defense Preparations

Military moves NORAD to Cheyenne Mountain

New concerns are being raised that the nation's electrical grid and critical infrastructure are increasingly vulnerable to a catastrophic foreign attack -- amid speculation over whether officials are eyeing a former Cold War bunker, inside a Colorado mountain, as a *shield* against such a strike.

The North American Aerospace Defense Command is looking for ways to protect itself in the event of a massive EMP. A $700 million contract with Raytheon to upgrade electronics inside Colorado's Cheyenne Mountain facility may provide a clue about just how worried the military is about the threat.

The Cheyenne Mountain bunker is a half-acre cavern carved into a mountain in the 1960s that was designed to withstand a Soviet nuclear attack. From inside the massive complex, airmen were poised to send warnings that could trigger the launch of nuclear missiles.

The Air Force moved out of Cheyenne Mountain, which was built to survive a nuclear attack, in 2006, establishing its NORAD headquarters at Peterson Air Force Base in Colorado. But that facility, inside the mountain, could offer protection against a so-called EMP attack.

The head of NORAD recently suggested, at an April 2015 Pentagon press conference, that Cheyenne may still be needed. "My primary concern was, are we going to have the space inside the mountain for everybody who wants to move in there?" Admiral William Gortney told reporters, "I'm not at liberty to discuss who's moving in there, but we do have that capability to be there. And so, there's a lot of movement to put capability into Cheyenne Mountain and to be able to communicate in there."

NORAD spokesman Capt. Jeff Davis, told Fox News, "The mountain's ability to provide a shield against an EMP is certainly a valuable feature, and that is one reason we maintain the ability to return there quickly, if needed."

Now, officials say that the Pentagon is looking at shifting communications gear to the Cheyenne bunker.

"A lot of the back office communications is being moved there," said one defense official.

Officials agree that the military's dependence on computer networks and digital communications makes it much more vulnerable to an electromagnetic pulse, which can occur naturally or result from a high-altitude nuclear explosion.

Under the 10-year contract, Raytheon is supposed to deliver "sustainment" services to help the military perform "accurate, timely, and unambiguous warning and attack assessment of air, missile, and space threats" at the Cheyenne and Peterson bases.

Raytheon's contract also involves unspecified work at Vandenberg Air Force Base in California and Offutt Air Force Base in Nebraska.

Pentagon constructs $44 million EMP-proof bunker in Alaska

Fort Greely, Alaska is home to one of America's two domestic missile defense bases. Now, it's getting armored against high-altitude electromagnetic energy attacks—like the kind emitted from nuclear blasts. The Pentagon is spending millions on a bunker designed to protect against exactly that. According to contract documents from the Army Corps of Engineers, the military plans to spend $44 million on an "HEMP-protected" bunker housing the base's missile launch control systems. The base at Fort Greely houses anti-ballistic missile interceptors stored in silos, and can also control and direct interceptors fired from a similar site at Vandenberg Air Force Base in California.

The sum allocated to the Fort Greely project is small in comparison to the $41 billion the Pentagon is spending on its ground-based defense program through FY2017. The plan calls for the installation of dozens of missile interceptors in Alaska and California. These interceptors will carry kinetic kill weapons, designed to impact and destroy ballistic missiles during their mid-course phase. Mid-course defense refers to the flight pattern of ballistic missiles as they travel through space—and before they reenter the atmosphere moving at extremely high speeds.

But a missile defense site wouldn't count for much if it could be knocked out by an EMP. The Pentagon is concerned enough with that scenario to protect its missile defense site. "The EMP and blast-proof building design also will provide a blueprint for subsequent launch-control buildings at Fort Greely," reported the trade journal, Military and Aerospace Electronics. Naturally, EMP-shielding also protects against lightning strikes, so it's a good insurance policy to shield the base's critical launch systems, in any case.

The contract points out that when the military first constructed the silos, the building housing the key launch components, "was not blast protected, HEMP shielded, and did not provide the utility redundancy to support a deployed weapons system." By protecting the base from EMP blasts, the Pentagon means the ability, "to resist the effects of a surface blast due to the accidental explosion of a missile as it exits a silo."

What are the United States government and the military preparing for? Why are they finally taking the threat seriously?

PART SIX
THE AFTERMATH

CRITICAL INFRASTRUCTURE – EVERYDAY ELECTRONICS

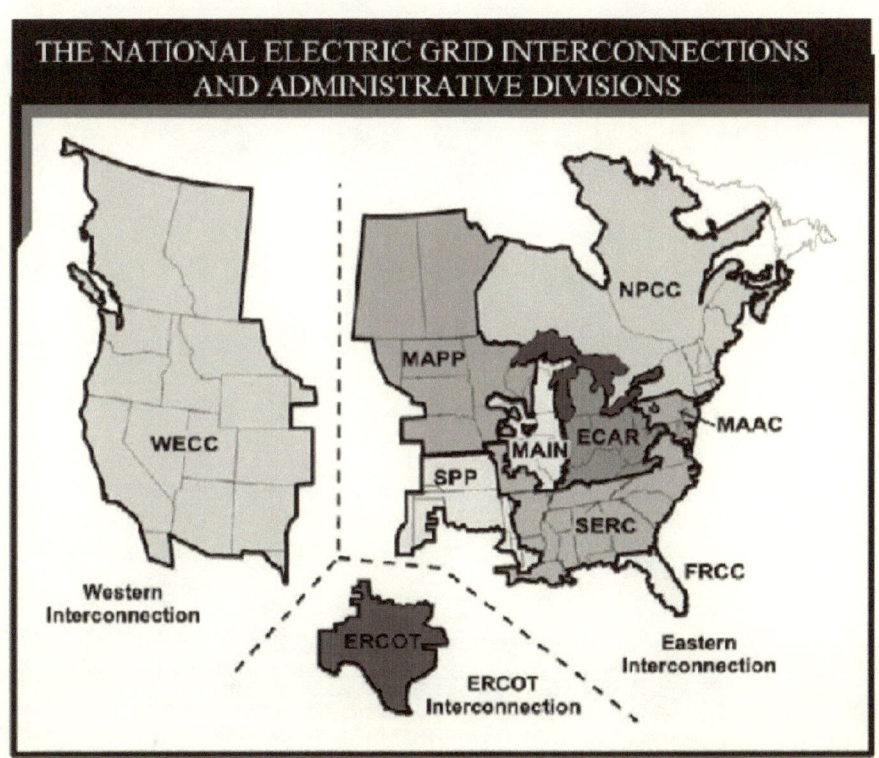

Organization of the national electric gird – the keystone critical infrastructure upon which all other infrastructures depend. (Source: EMP Commission, *Critical National Infrastructures*, p. 25.)

CHAPTER FIFTEEN
A COLLAPSE EVENT

In any extreme situation, you cannot survive for more than 3 minutes without air – 3 hours without shelter – 3 days without water – 3 weeks without food.

A collapse of the power grid may occur due to a cyber attack or an electromagnetic pulse. An EMP would destroy critical electrical infrastructure and potentially shut down a large portion of the nation's electrical grid. The widespread, functional collapse of the electric power system in the area affected by EMP would be likely.

But even if the U.S. is never attacked by an EMP weapon, scientists tell us that it is inevitable that a massive solar storm will fry our electrical grid someday. If an event similar to the solar storm of 1859—the Carrington Event—happened today, it would be catastrophic. That massive solar storm fried telegraph machines all over Europe and North America. At some point, we will experience another solar storm, and some scientists believe that we are already 50 years overdue for another one. In fact, the earth barely dodged a signficant CME in the summer of 2012.

Within 24 – 48 hours after the collapse of the power grid, lack of information will lead to confusion among the general population as traditional news acquisition sources like television, radio, and cell phone networks will be non-functional. Once people realize the power might not be coming back on, and grocery store shelves start emptying, the entire system will begin to delve into chaos. Within thirty days, mass casualties would begin as food supplies dwindled, looters and gangs turned to violent extremes, medicine couldn't be restocked and water pump stations failed.

What about long-term?

According to the EMP Commission that investigated this issue, approximately two-thirds of the U.S. population could potentially die from starvation, disease and societal chaos within one year. It would be a disaster, unlike anything that we have ever seen before in U.S. history.

Frank Gaffney, the president of the Center for Security Policy, is even more pessimistic. He believes that a single EMP blast could potentially end up killing almost the entire population of the United States.

"Within a year of that attack, nine out of 10 Americans would be dead because we can't support a population of the present size in urban centers and the like without electricity," Gaffney states.

As a society, we are simply not equipped to function without electricity. Dr. William Graham was the chairman of the government commission, which I mentioned above, and he believes that a Super-EMP blast could knock the United States back into "the late 1800s" in just a single moment.

Life after an EMP attack, "would probably be something that you might imagine life to be like around the late 1800s but with several times the population we had in those days, and without the ability of the country to support and sustain all those people," Graham says. "They wouldn't have power. Food supplies would be greatly taken out by the lack of transportation, telecommunication, power for refrigeration and so on."

If a direct solar flare hits the earth, some of which can be 14 times the size of our planet, scientists from NASA and the National Academy of Sciences say it would cost the nation up to $2 trillion in the first year. It could take four to ten years to recover and would affect ninety percent of the U.S. population, meaning widespread starvation and death.

CHAPTER SIXTEEN
CRITICAL INFRASTRUCTURE

EMP: A Threat from Above to America's Soft Underbelly Below

How will America survive a complete collapse of our critical infrastructure following an EMP attack?

The clock is ticking. One Second After. One Year After. Even if there is never a major EMP attack against the United States, scientists tell us that it is only a matter of time before a massive solar storm fries the electrical grid.

An EMP event could knock out the U.S. electrical grid system and the critical infrastructures that rely on it. Along with the national electrical grid, other critical infrastructures include telecommunications, banking and financial transactions, oil and natural gas pipelines, transportation, food and water delivery, emergency services and space systems.

And without a doubt, our electrical grid represents the "soft underbelly" of the U.S. infrastructure.

Critical infrastructure is the backbone of every nations' economy, security, and health. It is the power we use in our homes, the water we drink, the transportation that moves us, and the communication systems that we rely on to stay in touch with friends and family. Critical infrastructure includes the assets, systems, and networks, whether physical or virtual, so vital to a country that its incapacitation or destruction would have a debilitating effect on security, national economic security, national public health or safety, or any combination thereof.

The following lists twelve examples of critical infrastructure that are highly sensitive and vulnerable to EMP attacks:

- Electricity generation/production, transmission and distribution, Electrical Grids and Smart Grid Systems
- Gasoline production, transport, and distribution
- Heating (gas, fuel oil, steam, etc.)
- Satellite and land-based telecommunication; network, transmission and control centers
- Mobile communications network, base stations and centers
- Data centers; data equipment, control centers, power supply, cooling, etc.
- Transportation systems (fuel supply for vehicles, railway network, airports, harbors, inland shipping)
- Financial services (stock exchange, banking, ATMs, etc.)
- Agriculture food production and distribution
- Water supply (drinking water, waste water/sewage, stemming of surface water)
- Public health (hospitals, ambulances, mental health facilities)
- Security services (FEMA, police, military, prison system)

Most infrastructures have data/telecom systems highly dependent on critical electronic systems and equipment including power systems, cooling, vents. etc. Telecommunications systems, modern vehicles, and more, have vulnerable electronic devices and processors that are highly sensitive to an EMP. All unprotected electronic systems and equipment have a high possibility for a temporary or permanent failure after an EMP event.

The effect of an EMP attack is not limited to electronics on Earth. Satellite systems can be hit by an EMP, (Solar storms, HEMP explosion, etc.) and indirectly cause massive problems for various transportation and telecom systems like airline and ship traffic, on-land transportation, and mobile phone networks.

Experts call the North American power grid *the largest machine in the world.* Its massive scale and reach make it impossible to protect fully. However, this vulnerability doesn't leave us defenseless. It does just the opposite. Due to its distributed nature and extensive network, the grid is phenomenally resilient, with the ability to shift power distribution at any time of day, and seal off potential areas of concern or damage. Likewise, working in the power industry, grid owners and operators have agreements in place to immediately deploy needed personnel and resources, identify and deliver spare equipment, including large transformers, and initiate recovery efforts to restore power quickly.

But what if the power grid comes under a sustained, coordinated attack? The concept of rolling blackouts concerns FERC and utility companies nationwide. It has already happened in America on several occasions. The extensive network was unable to pick up the slack as envisioned.

To their credit, power utilities are always reviewing ways to strengthen the nation's critical infrastructure. The North American Electric Reliability Corporation and FERC are working together to enhance reliability as it relates to geomagnetic disturbances as well. Naturally occurring solar storms could also impact the electric grid. NERC and FERC have developed standards requiring emergency procedures and preparedness strategies that would mitigate the effects of a significant geomagnetic storm event. Regulators and scientists at NERC recognize that these two events, EMPs and geomagnetic storms, are often incorrectly equated with one another. An EMP produces destructive energy pulses significantly more damaging than those created by a solar event, but mitigation measures applied for an EMP event can enhance protection.

America's critical infrastructure can never be completely secured from all potential dangers, including terrorist attacks and cyber intrusions, but the power industry is managing the EMP threat in tangible and consistent ways. With every incident, including significant geomagnetic storms, the industry is learning — and the grid is getting better-equipped to handle evolving threats. This knowledge creates a compounding effect of lessons learned, that ultimately helps the sector meet challenges presented by many threats, including EMPs.

Targeted attacks on the electrical grid happen all the time, but most of them are not reported by the mainstream media. The following report of an attack is from 2013:

More than 10,000 people in Arkansas were dumped into a blackout in 2013 following an attack on that state's electric grid, The FBI announced that in August of 2013, a major transmission line in the region, around Cabot, Arkansas, was deliberately cut. Also, they said that two power poles had been intentionally cut in Lonoke County, resulting in an outage.

The following is how the FBI described the attack:

In the early morning hours of September 29, 2013, officials with Entergy Arkansas reported a fire at its Keo substation located on Arkansas Highway 165 between Scott and England, in Lonoke County. Fortunately, there were no injuries and no reported power outages. The investigation has determined that the fire, which consumed the control house at the substation, was intentionally set. The person or persons responsible for this incident inscribed a message on a metal control panel outside the substation which reads, "YOU SHOULD HAVE EXPECTED US."

The FBI did not label this a terrorist attack, although some analysts believe this could have been a trial run for a bigger intrusion. But minor attacks like that are nothing compared to what an EMP weapon could potentially do to our electrical grid.

Also, radio frequency weapons are so simple that terror groups could easily build them and use them. Any individual with a penchant for electronics can pull together components from a Radio Shack or electronic store – even order the components off of selected websites – and construct a radio frequency weapon.

As microprocessors become smaller but more sophisticated, they are even more susceptible to an RF pulse. The microwave from an

RF weapon produces a short, very high power pulse, said to be billions of watts in a nanosecond, or one billionth of a second. This so-called burst of electromagnetic waves in the gigahertz microwave frequency band can melt electrical circuitry and damage integrated circuits, causing them to fail.

Constructing a radio frequency weapon is not difficult at all. In fact, you can find instructions on how to build them online.

In the future, hand-held electromagnetic weapons are going to become even more powerful and even easier to use. Meanwhile, we are going to continue to become even more dependent on electricity and technology.

CHAPTER SEVENTEEN
EFFECTS ON PEOPLE

So what would life look like for you and your family if this happened? Consider the following:

- There would be no heat or air-conditioning for your home.

- Water would no longer be pumped into most homes.

- Your computer would not work; neither would the internet because both Cable and Telephones would be inoperative.

- There would be no television or radio.

- ATMs would shut down, and there would be no banking or credit card transactions.

- Without electricity, gas stations would not be functioning.

- Most people would be unable to do their jobs without power and employment would collapse, bringing the economy to a standstill.

- Hospitals would not be able to function, and a nation heavily dependent upon prescription medication would have to do without.

- All refrigeration would shut down, and frozen foods in our homes and supermarkets would spoil.

- Most vehicles would become inoperable, and traffic lights would no longer be working.

- Airplanes would be grounded.

- Wall Street would shut down.

- Most Government services would collapse.

After an EMP attack, the consequences of a grid down scenario would be felt immediately. However, other than the loss of conveniences and use of technology to which many have grown accustomed, you would not feel any physical effects of the EMP. In fact, other than the resulting power outages, you wouldn't know that it had occurred.

The best current estimate is that the electromagnetic pulse (EMP) produced by a high altitude nuclear detonation is not likely to have direct adverse effects on people. An important exception is people whose well-being depends on electronic life-support equipment. They would be directly impacted by the electromagnetic pulse that disrupts or damages such devices. Research sponsored by the EMP Commission suggests that some heart pacemakers might be among the devices susceptible to damage from a high-altitude EMP.

While most of the effects on people would be indirect, the impact could be significant in a just-in-time economy, in which local stocks of medicines, food, and other health-critical items are limited. The physical consequences of a high-altitude EMP attack would likely include the failure of the electric power grid and the degradation of telecommunication systems, computers, and electronic components over large areas of the country. A disruption of this scale could cripple critical infrastructures and hinder the delivery of day-to-day necessities, because of the interconnectivity of telecommunication networks and the electrical dependence of most cities, government agencies, businesses, households, and individuals. It also could require a long recovery period. To assess human consequences, the contingency of concern is one in which electricity, telecommunications, and electronics are out of service over a significant area for an extended period.

The human consequences of such a scenario include the social and psychological reactions to a sudden loss of stability in the modern infrastructure over a large area of the country. Lack of information would be a contributing factor to the resulting societal collapse in a grid down scenario. Americans would be in shock initially, and might even deny that the power grid could be down for a significant time. After a period of anger, the population would become scared, and then desperate. Opportunists would rise to take advantage of the situation—a society without the rule of law.

Our politicians are unwilling to admit this, but the biggest threat to America is not the EMP attack itself, but the resulting societal collapse. Unfortunately, what one should fear the most is their fellow man.

Impact of an EMP Attack

While no single event serves as a model for an EMP scenario with the incidence of a long-lasting widespread power outage, communications failure, and other effects, the combined analysis by the EMP Commission of the following case studies, provides useful insight in determining human reactions following an EMP attack. From the EMP Commission:

Blackouts:

- Northeast (1965)

- New York (1977)

- Hydro Quebec (1989)

- Western states (1996)

- Auckland, New Zealand (1998)

- Northeast (2003)

Natural Disasters: NOTE: Add Katrina and Sandy, remove Midwest floods!!!!!

- Hurricane Hugo (1989)

- Hurricane Andrew (1992)

- Midwest floods (1993)

Terrorist Incidents:

- World Trade Center attack (2001)

- Anthrax attacks (2001)

Blackouts

In 1965, a blackout occurred over the northeastern United States and parts of Canada. New Hampshire; Vermont; Massachusetts; Connecticut; Rhode Island; New York, including metropolitan New York City; and a small part of Pennsylvania were in the dark after operators at Consolidated Edison were forced to shut down its generators to avoid damage. Street traffic was chaotic, and some people were trapped in elevators, but there were few instances of antisocial behavior while the lights were out. It was a "long night in the dark," but the recovery proceeded without incident, and citizens experienced relative civility.

TIME Magazine described New York's next blackout, in 1977, as a "Night of Terror." Widespread chaos reigned in the city until power was restored — entire blocks were looted and set ablaze, people flipped over cars and vans on the streets; the city was in pandemonium. That night 3,776 arrests were made, and certainly not all looters, thieves, and arsonists were apprehended or arrested. While this is a dramatic example of antisocial behavior following a blackout, sociologists point to extraordinary demographic and historical issues that contributed to the looting. For instance, extreme poverty and socioeconomic inequality plagued New York neighborhoods, and many of the looters originated from the poorer sections of the city, engaging in "vigilante redistribution" by looting consumer goods and luxuries. Racial tensions were high, and a serial killer known as Son of Sam had recently terrorized New Yorkers.

In 1989, more than six million customers lost power when a geomagnetic storm caused a massive power failure in Quebec. The electricity failures resulting from this geomagnetic storm reached a much larger area than is typically affected by traditional blackouts resulting from technological failure. However, the outage lasted just over nine hours, most of which were during the day. Local and national papers were curiously silent about the blackout, and little to no unusual or adverse human behavior was attributed to the power loss. The event was most significantly a lesson for operators of the North American electric grids because it revealed vulnerabilities in the system.

In 1998, Auckland, New Zealand, experienced a significant blackout that lasted more than five weeks and affected more than one million people. Civility reigned for the duration of the outage, which was likely attributed to a number of factors, including:

- There was no significant threat to public health because water and sewage infrastructures were functioning.

- In anticipation of potential incidents, police increased their presence in urban areas.

- The recovery process was underway nearly immediately, communicating to the public that the situation would eventually be under control.

- Nearly all blackout recovery resources of New Zealand were rushed to the capital for recovery efforts.

Recovery efforts from elsewhere in New Zealand were significant, symbolically as well as practically, as demonstrated by the fact that electricity was available elsewhere. Businesses attempted to carry on as normally as possible. Social consequences included criticism and blame of the authorities, both municipal and national because the technological failures were attributed in large part to the privatization of the power sector. However, this response never materialized into violence, crime, or social disorder.

Most recently, New York City and the eight states in the Northeast experienced another significant blackout in August 2003. While the blackout inconvenienced many on a hot summer day, general civility remained intact. News coverage indicated that those affected by the blackout dealt with the obstacles quietly and even developed a sort of camaraderie, while struggling through nights without running water and electricity. In contrast to the 1977 power outage, police made only 850 arrests the night of the 2003 blackout, of which "only 250 to 300 were directly attributable to the blackout," indicating a slight decline from the average number of arrests on a given summer day. While this blackout was widespread, it was not long lasting, and it did not interrupt the communications infrastructure significantly.

Blackouts provide only a partial picture of life following an EMP attack. Most blackouts are localized and are resolved quickly. Further, usually communication systems are not completely shut down, and major infrastructures can remain intact if significant portions of infrastructure hardware are located outside of the affected area. To best approximate the effects of longer-lasting, widespread infrastructure disruption—with or without electrical power failure—it is necessary to look to natural disasters for examples of human reaction.

Natural Disasters

At the time that Hurricane Hugo hit in 1989, it was the most intense hurricane to strike the coastline of Georgia and the Carolinas in over one-hundred years. Hurricane Hugo's survivors indicate that some individuals, who suffered personal and financial losses from the hurricane, showed clinically significant symptoms of psychological trauma. According to some researchers, many of the adverse mental health effects of Hugo could be explained by deterioration in perceived social support. Overall, the rate of post-traumatic stress disorder symptoms was low, but stress effects lingered long after the hurricane's physical damage was repaired.

Hurricane Andrew cut a wide path across Florida and along the coast of the Gulf of Mexico in 1992, causing $26.5 billion in damage. Andrew left 250,000 families homeless and 1.4 million families without electricity immediately following the hurricane.

After such extraordinary destruction and disruption, it is perhaps not surprising that one-third of a sample of individuals met criteria for post-traumatic stress disorder four months after the hurricane.

Hurricanes Hugo and Andrew demonstrated to psychologists that disaster-related declines in perceived support explained the difference in symptoms between the two disasters; deterioration was more significant in Andrew and the recovery was weaker. In the long-lasting recovery period, Floridians saw looting, opportunism, and vigilante civil defense. Press coverage of Hurricane Andrew suggests that after a multi-state disaster, people will expect help, and they will expect it from the federal government, as well as from state and local authorities.

Flooding in the Midwest in 1993 resulted in twenty-five deaths, affected more than 8 million acres, cost billions of dollars in property damage and more than 2 billion dollars in crop damage. Water depths ranged from eleven feet of flooding in Minneapolis to forty-three feet of flooding in St. Louis. Electricity was restored, where possible, within three days and in downtown Des Moines within 23 hours. The floods devastated families, businesses, and individuals, who lost nearly everything and were unable to control events throughout the recovery process. Thousands of people assisted in volunteer recovery efforts by sandbagging and providing needed supplies. Most came from unaffected areas to help the most urgent victims. The flooding provides an example of widespread damage crippling several infrastructures for a significant period, and an example of a disaster in which regional experience may matter tremendously in disaster recovery.

Blackouts and natural disasters have limits as approximations of recovery following an EMP attack. An important element is the relevance of fear and individual panic in these situations versus what might occur following an EMP attack. For this component, it is useful to examine recent terrorist incidents in the United States to gauge the effects of fear for the public. Because terrorist attacks appear to be indiscriminate and random, they can arouse acute anxiety and feelings of helplessness, which shatter beliefs of invulnerability and even a belief in justice and order in the world.

Terrorist Incidents

The attacks on the World Trade Center in New York on September 11, 2001, certainly qualify as seemingly indiscriminate and random. Following this disaster, in which nearly 3,000 people died, those in the immediate and surrounding area showed considerable psychological trauma and damage. Some individuals who experienced these attacks may have lost confidence in their abilities to cope and control outcomes. Overall, however, the survivors of the attacks proved remarkably resilient, flexible, and competent in the face of an arbitrary, violent, and completely unexpected attack.

In October 2001, a month following the attack on the World Trade Center, Americans saw a series of anthrax-infected mail pieces, threatening intended mail recipients and handlers. The death toll was small (five individuals), but public concern was considerable.

This period is an example of an open response to an adversary-initiated threat that disrupted infrastructure. The public demonstrated a great need for control over the situation, through preparedness and information. For example, many Americans took protective measures, despite the astronomical odds against infection. The news media was saturated with reports of anthrax infections, suspected infections, and general information about anthrax and how to respond to infection. Though no culprit was apprehended, the attacks stopped, and normal postal activity resumed.

Some Lessons Learned

Though the United States has not experienced a severe, widespread disruption to infrastructure comparable to an EMP attack, the cases reviewed provide some practical direction for predictions of behavior. For example, it can be expected that emotional reactions such as shock and paralysis that have followed past disasters could be magnified in a large-scale event such as an EMP attack. In particular, the paralysis of government assistance entities, such as law enforcement and emergency services, would aggravate this effect.

In most instances, social disorder would be minimal, in significant part, due to the knowledge that authorities are in control of the situation. Without that assurance from an outside source, it appears likely that people would turn to immediate neighbors or community members for information and support, if possible.

Following disruptive disasters, information is among the most pressing need for individuals. Not surprisingly, people's first concerns are the whereabouts and safety of their family members and friends. Another urgent priority is an understanding of the situation — knowledge of what has happened, who and what is affected, and the cause of the situation. A related yet distinct information need is for confirmation that the situation will be resolved, either by common sense and experience, in the case of a small-scale disaster, or from the involvement of local or federal authorities, in the event of a large-scale disaster. Psychologists note that dramatic events force people to reexamine their fundamental understanding of the world and that survivors need to process an event before they can fully absorb it. This information processing begins the alternating phases of intrusion and avoidance that are primary indicators of post-traumatic stress.

The aftermath of natural disasters is often marked by a period of considerable pro-social behavior such as cooperation, social solidarity, and acts of selflessness. However, this encouraging observation might not be similarly magnified in projections for human behavior following an EMP attack. The key, intangible, immeasurable difference is the knowledge that normal order would resume, based on significant indicators. It is important to note some of the differences between natural disasters and technological disasters, particularly those caused by human intent. Natural disasters "create a social context marked by an initial overwhelming consensus regarding priorities and the allocation of resources," which explains the enormous outpouring of voluntary support following the floods of 1993. In contrast to natural disasters, which "occur as purposeless, asocial events; civil disturbances can be viewed as instrumentally initiated to achieve certain social goals." An EMP attack would certainly be perceived similarly, whether the adversary was a terrorist organization or a state.

The selected case studies by the EMP Commission provide only an approximation of EMP effects. For example, the impact of the knowledge that widespread infrastructure disruption resulted from an intentional foreign attack are yet unknown. Past evidence points to people's resilience in the immediate aftermath of disasters. However, during a lengthy recovery process, as would be expected following an EMP attack with widespread, long-duration effects, the psychological effects of the attack should not be underestimated.

It appears clear that the most crucial question in the task of avoiding societal collapse is how to provide information to the populace without electricity immediately following an EMP attack. Without communication alternatives, it would be impossible to alert people to the availability of emergency supplies or inform them concerning emergency response activities. It also appears clear that greater awareness of the nature of an EMP attack and knowledge of what prudent preparations might be undertaken to mitigate its consequences would be desirable. The EMP Commission made the following recommendations.

Recommendations

The EMP Commission arrived at several common sense suggestions, most importantly, involving measures to ensure that the President can communicate effectively with the citizenry. The following recommendations were made:

- Because many citizens would be without power, communications, and other services for a significant period of time before full recovery could occur, it will be crucial to provide a reliable channel of information to all Americans. In particular:

- The Department of Homeland Security should play a leading role in spreading knowledge of the nature of prudent mitigation preparations for EMP attack to mitigate its consequences.

- The Department of Homeland Security should add content to Web sites it maintains, such as www.Ready.gov, which provides concise overviews of the threats posed by EMP attacks and geomagnetic storms, summarizes steps that people should take given an incident and identifies alternate or emergency communications channels.

- The Department of Homeland Security should work with state homeland security organizations to develop and exercise communications networks involving the organizations that normally operate in each community.

After the EMP Commission's term expired in 2008, the sense of urgency regarding these simple suggestions began to fall off our lawmaker's radar. In 2015, that changed as the NDAA, for Fiscal Year 2016, revived the Commission. It is time to increase awareness, once again.

PART SEVEN
EMP SHIELDING – FARADAY CAGES

From the simplistic to the sophisticated

CHAPTER EIGHTEEN
MEET MICHAEL FARADAY

"Faraday is, and must always remain, the father of that enlarged science of electromagnetism."

~ James Clerk Maxwell, renowned Scottish Scientist

Michael Faraday, who came from a destitute family, became one of the greatest scientists in history. His achievement was remarkable, in a time when science was the preserve of people born into privileged households. His work may save all of our lives someday.

Inspiration

It was Ben Franklin who helped inspire many of the ideas behind Michael Faraday's scientific work. Franklin, of course, spent part of his illustrious career flying kites in thunderstorms in attempts to attract lightning and thus was already acquainted with the concepts of electricity.

In 1755, Franklin began toying with electricity in new ways. He electrified a silver pint can and dropped an uncharged cork ball attached to a non-conductive silk thread into it. He lowered the ball until it touched the bottom of the can and observed that the ball wasn't attracted to the interior sides of the can. Yet when Franklin withdrew the cork ball and dangled it near the electrified can's exterior, the ball was immediately drawn to the can's surface.

Franklin was mystified by the interplay of electricity and the charged and uncharged objects. He admitted as much in a letter to a colleague: "You require the reason; I do not know it. Perhaps you may discover it, and then you will be so good as to communicate it to me."

Decades later, an English physicist and chemist, named Michael

Faraday, made other pertinent observations -- namely, he realized that an electrical conductor—such as a metal cage—when charged, exhibited that charge only on its surface. It had no effect on the interior of the conductor.

Education and Early Life

Michael Faraday was born on September 22, 1791, in London, England, UK. He was the third child of James and Margaret Faraday. His father was a blacksmith who endured ill health. Before marriage, his mother had been a servant. The family lived in a degree of poverty.

Faraday attended a local school until he was thirteen, where he received a basic education. To earn money for the family, he started working as a delivery boy for a bookshop. He worked hard and impressed his employer. After a year, he was promoted to become an apprentice bookbinder.

Faraday was eager to learn more about the world; he did not restrict himself to binding the shop's books. After working hard each day, he spent his free time reading the books he had bound. Gradually, he found he was reading more and more about science. Two books, in particular, captivated him:

- *The Encyclopedia Britannica* – his source for electrical knowledge and much more

- *Conversations on Chemistry* – 600 pages of chemistry for ordinary people written by Jane Marcet

He became so fascinated, that he started spending part of his meager pay on chemicals and apparatus to confirm the truth of what he was reading. He immersed himself in the world of chemistry and science. He took notes and then made so many additions to the notes that he produced a 300-page handwritten book, which he bound and distributed.

At this time, Faraday had begun more sophisticated experiments at the back of the bookshop, building an electric battery using copper coins and zinc discs, separated by moist, salty paper. He used his battery to decompose chemicals—such as magnesium sulfate. A scientist was born.

Faraday's Scientific Achievements and Discoveries

It would be easy to fill a book with details of all of Faraday's discoveries – in both chemistry and physics. It is no accident that Albert Einstein used to keep photographs of three scientists in his office: Isaac Newton, James Clerk Maxwell and Michael Faraday. Faraday was a man devoted to discovery through experimentation, and he was famous for never giving up on any ideas that came from his scientific intuition. If he thought an idea was a good one, Faraday would keep experimenting through multiple failures until he achieved the desired result, or until he finally decided that Mother Nature had shown his intuition to be wrong. History would prove that in Faraday's case, this was rare.

Here are some of his most notable discoveries:

1821: Discovery of Electromagnetic Rotation

This was a glimpse of what would eventually develop into the electric motor, based on Hans Christian Oersted's discovery that a wire carrying electric current has magnetic properties.

1823: Gas Liquefaction—the conversion of a gas into a liquid state, and subsequent refrigeration of gas

1825: Discovery of Benzene

Historically benzene is one of the most important substances in chemistry, both in a practical sense – i.e. making new materials, and in a theoretical sense – i.e. understanding chemical bonding. Faraday discovered benzene in the oily residue left behind from producing gas for lighting during his days in London.

1831: Discovery of Electromagnetic Induction

This was an enormously important discovery for the future of both science and technology. Faraday discovered that a varying magnetic field caused electricity to flow through an electric circuit. For example, moving a horseshoe magnet over a wire produces an electric current, because the movement of the magnet caused a varying magnetic field.

Previously, people had only been able to produce electric current with a battery. Now Faraday had shown that movement could be turned into electricity – or in more scientific language, kinetic energy could be converted into electrical energy. Most of the power in our homes today is produced using this principle. Rotation, kinetic energy, is converted into electricity using electromagnetic induction. The rotation can be generated by high-pressure steam from coal, gas, or nuclear energy turning turbines, by hydroelectric plants, and by wind-turbines.

1834: Faraday's Laws of Electrolysis

Faraday was one of the major players in the founding of the science of electrochemistry—what happens at the interface of an electrode with an ionic substance. Electrochemistry is the science that has produced the Lithium-ion battery and the metal hydride battery, both capable of powering modern mobile technology. Faraday's laws are vital to our understanding of electrode reactions.

1836: Invention of the Faraday Cage

Faraday discovered that when an electrical conductor becomes charged, all of the extra charge sits on the outside of the conductor. This means that the additional charge does not appear on the inside of a room or cage made of metal. In addition to offering protection for people, sensitive electrical or electrochemical experiments can be placed inside a Faraday Cage to prevent interference from the external electrical activity. Faraday cages can also create dead zones for mobile communications.

1845: Discovery of the Faraday Effect – a magneto-optical effect

This was another vital experiment in the history of science. Faraday was the first to link electromagnetism and light – a link finally described fully by James Clerk Maxwell's equations in 1864, which established that light is an electromagnetic wave. Faraday discovered that a magnetic field causes the plane of light polarization to rotate.

Michael Faraday died in London, aged 75, on August 25, 1867. He was survived by his wife, Sarah. They had no children. He had been a devout Christian all of his life.

He will be remembered by the following quote:

Nature is our kindest friend and best critic in experimental science if we only

allow her intimations to fall unbiased on our minds.

Pieter Zeeman, 1902 Nobel Prize in Physics, wrote about Faraday when recalling the two titles of Faraday's fundamental work: *Magnetization of light* and *Illumination of lines of force.*

"They appear to us to be almost prophesies, because we have now seen that light can in fact be magnetized, and in nature itself, in the northern lights, an example of illumination of the magnetic lines of force of the Earth by the electrons escaping from the sun."

Prophetic indeed.

Chapter Nineteen
Introduction to the Faraday Cage

A Faraday cage or Faraday shield is an enclosure formed by conductive material or by a mesh of such material, used to block electric fields. Faraday cages sometimes go by other names. They can be called Faraday boxes, RF (radio frequency) shields, or EMF (electromotive force) cages. No matter what you call them, Faraday cages are most often used in scientific labs, either in experiments or product development.

A Faraday cage operates because an external electrical field causes the electric charges within the cage's conducting material to be distributed such that they cancel the field's effect in the cage's interior. This phenomenon is used to protect sensitive electronic equipment from external radio frequency interference. Faraday cages are also used to enclose devices that produce radio frequencies, such as radio transmitters, to prevent their radio waves from interfering with other nearby equipment. They are also used to protect people and equipment against actual electric currents, such as lightning strikes and electrostatic discharges, since the cage conducts the electric current around the outside of the enclosed space and none passes through to the interior.

Faraday cages cannot block static or slowly varying magnetic fields, such as the Earth's magnetic field (a compass will still work inside). To a large degree, though, they shield the interior from external electromagnetic radiation if the conductor is thick enough and any holes are significantly smaller than the wavelength of the radiation. For example, certain computer forensic test procedures of electronic systems that require an environment free of electromagnetic interference can be carried out within a screened room. These are separate spaces that are completely enclosed by one or more layers of a fine metal mesh or perforated sheet metal. The metal layers are grounded to dissipate any electric currents generated from external or internal electromagnetic fields. Thus, they block a large amount of the electromagnetic interference.

A Faraday cage is designed to protect against an electromagnetic pulse that may be the result of a high-altitude nuclear detonation resulting in an EMP. A Faraday cage protects electronics by three different principles:

- the conductive layer reflects incoming fields

- the conductor absorbs incoming energy

- the cage acts to create opposing fields.

In concert, these principles safeguard the contents from excessive energy levels.

For most geomagnetic storms, a Faraday cage is not necessary to protect against the size and scope of the most common coronal mass ejections because solar disturbances are at much lower, E3-level frequencies. A solar event doesn't transfer energy in sufficient amounts into small electronics, except through wires coming into the system, which act as an antenna. A simple precaution against solar events is to unplug electronics or use high-quality surge suppressors.

Faraday cages may have holes as long as they are small. This is why fine conductive/shielding fabric can be used when constructing a Faraday cage. In practice, the cage's lid or door usually causes the most leakage. Taping the seam with aluminum tape prevents gaps. The gaps and seams must remain tiny for the item to be effective.

A lot has been written about the grounding of a Faraday cage. The grounding of the cage, by attaching it to a steel rod driven into the earth, has little effect on the field levels seen inside the Faraday cage itself. Grounding primarily helps to keep the cage from becoming charged and perhaps re-radiating. In practice, an ungrounded Faraday cage protects the contents from harmful electromagnetic pulses as well as a grounded one.

Some experts argue that grounding your Faraday cage is a bad idea. Although EMPs and lightning strikes are very different regarding intensity, you might consider how lightning strikes affect a flying plane. The metal shell of the aircraft acts as a giant Faraday cage, dispersing the electromagnetic energy around the plane. The airplane isn't grounded. Therefore the effects of lightning strikes are minimal.

A recent invention, the anti-static bag, is readily available to protect electronic components against EMPs. They can be purchased in many different sizes, including some large enough to hold radio equipment. Dr. Arthur T. Bradley, author and recognized preparedness expert, opined that while they do offer shielding from EMP, not all products are created equal. He found testing confirmed that products certified to MIL-PRF-8170 and/or MIL-PRF-131 provide the greatest protection from an EMP. Further, when selecting an anti-static bag, consider not only the shielding effectiveness, but also the physical ruggedness of the bag. A tear or large hole can compromise the bag by allowing EMP energy to enter.

Storing a larger set of electronics might require a closet or more considerable space. A DIY shield room can be made by lining a small closet with conductive/shielding mesh, covering the entire room, and then sealing the gaps left by the entry with aluminum tape.

There are three principal methods of protecting vulnerable electronic devices from a damaging EMP attack and natural EMP events;

- Put equipment in a shielded room based on Faraday Cage principles

- Hide it deep into mountain plants or underground bunkers

- Place it in the center of a substantial building behind thick reinforced concrete walls and roof – primarily underground.

The first alternative typically gives necessary protection, assuming that correct and solid construction is met.

The protection effectiveness in a mountain plant or bunker depends on several factors like type of rock and soil, the degree of coverage, cable length, protection devices like gates and other barriers in front of the tunnel, etc.

The last alternative gives only a limited level of protection and is normally not sufficient unless it's combined with additional solutions; like a Faraday Cage.

Chapter Twenty
Construct a Simple Faraday Cage

The primary method to protect electronic equipment from lightning strikes, electrostatic discharges and EMP is the Faraday Cage. For the majority of household electronics, such as audio-visual, communication, or appliances that can be unplugged from their power source, a Faraday Cage is the easiest way of protecting the smallest electrical equipment. Generally speaking, a Faraday Cage could be a metal box, a trash can, or a manufactured mesh structure designed to divert the electromagnetic pulse. It is important that the objects placed inside the Faraday Cage be insulated from the inside surface of the box, ensuring the object will not be affected by the electronic pulse traveling around the outside metal surface of the box.

A simple and inexpensive design can be achieved through DIY containers suitable for most Faraday Cage purposes. Some examples include cookie tins, ammunition cans, microwave ovens, metal filing cabinets, and galvanized steel trash cans. Faraday Cages do NOT have to be airtight, due to the long wavelength of an electromagnetic pulse. However, the design of the Faraday Cage using a conductive mesh needs to be impeccable. A Faraday Cage can be made of wire screen or other porous metal and provide the necessary protection for your devices.

To construct a simple Faraday Cage using a galvanized trash can, you can follow the step-by-step instructions found on our website: FreedomPreppers.com. Here are the basics.

The primary requirements for protection when designing a Faraday Cage are:

- The electrical equipment inside the box cannot touch the metal container. Insulating with foam, cardboard, rubber, plastic or even wads of paper are acceptable methods.

- The metal shielding must be continuous. There can be no large holes or gaps in the shielding material.

Now that you understand the basic principles let's apply them to a simple Faraday Cage for home use.

There are a few decisions you have to make before starting your homemade Faraday Cage:

- The shape. The cage can have any shape you like: spherical, triangular, oddly shaped, and so on. If you decide to go with the classic rectangular shape, that's acceptable, as long as you know that the shape doesn't affect the cage's effectiveness. As always, keep it simple.

- The conductor material. You must choose the material you want to put on the outside of the cage. This should be a simple decision, as the material doesn't influence the cage's activity (as long as it is capable to conduct electricity as discussed above). A heavy-duty, galvanized trash can be the most cost-effective material for an efficient DIY Faraday Cage.

- Holes or no holes. A Faraday Cage can have holes in its walls as long as they are not too big to let the electromagnetic wave in. That's why you can use an aluminum mesh as the outer layer of the cage. However, don't risk a design flaw. After an EMP attack, you don't get a do-over. Use a galvanized trash can and seal the lid with aluminum tape. Make sure the lid is secured firmly to the garbage can.

- Cushioning material. Use a variety of cushioning material to protect the electronics from the inside walls of the Faraday Cage. We suggest upholstery foam that can be purchased in rolls and cut to fit.

- Grounding the Faraday Cage. The debate will rage on regarding this requirement. It's not necessary, in our opinion.

- Protection against moisture. This is an often overlooked necessity. Moisture will ruin electronics. Your Faraday Cage must be moisture absorbent to create a safe and dry environment for the devices inside. They won't do you any good if they survive an EMP but they cease to function from moisture damage because of the excessive humidity. Add 50-gram desiccant packs to the inside before sealing.

Now that you've got everything you need, it's time to start building:

Begin by wrapping everything you want to put in the cage in a heavy duty aluminum foil. You can add a piece of cloth before putting on the foil if the object you're wrapping has sharp corners. Make sure you put at least two layers of aluminum foil on each item. It's important to cover tears or holes in the foil.

Take the container you are using as the walls of the Faraday Cage and add a protection layer on the inside. Here, you can use a foam cushion or simply a cut up cardboard box. The cushion will be a better protective layer, especially if you need to grab the trash can handle in an expedited bug-out situation. If you're not going to bang the cage against the walls, you should be fine with the cardboard box material. Make sure that you add this interior layer on the entire interior. The items inside cannot touch the walls of the container, especially if you're using a galvanized trash can.

Place the moisture absorbent desiccant packs, and the items you want to protect, inside the container.

Secure the lid and add an extra layer of aluminum tape around the seal. The layer of tape is just to make sure that the seal is made, and there are no intrusions between the metal contacts. For the cage to work, this seal must be perfect.

A final test is recommended. Unless you are prepared to construct your own radio frequency weapon, you can't produce an actual electromagnetic pulse to test the Faraday Cage you just built, but there are other ways to see if it is properly constructed. Place a portable AM/FM radio and turn up the volume so that it is loud. Before securing the lid in place you will still be able to hear the radio's signal from inside the container. After everything is sealed up, the radio should lose signal. If this happens, it means your Faraday Cage will protect your electronics. You can try the test with a cell phone as well. If your phone rings while inside the sealed cage, look for holes in the container or in the aluminum foil used to wrap the items.

Now that we know how to protect our electronics, it's time to learn a few alternative tips and techniques on how to create a Faraday Cage with materials at your disposal.

- Use nylon stockings filled with crystal cat litter to absorb the moisture inside. It's an inexpensive and effective alternative to make sure your Faraday Cage is moisture free.

- Pack your items and put them in the can in the order that you are going to need them. If there are items you need to check on regularly, put them at the top.

- You could embed a solar panel in a large Faraday cage to keep your electronics running even if the power lines are down. Some argue that a disconnected solar panel is not at risk. There is no definitive answer. Out of precaution, we shield ours.

- Keep your devices charged, and store charged batteries.

CHAPTER TWENTY-ONE
SOPHISTICATED SHIELDED ROOMS

Faraday Cages cannot block static or slowly varying magnetic fields, such as the Earth's magnetic field. To a large degree, though, they shield the interior from external electromagnetic radiation, if the conductor is thick enough and any holes are significantly smaller than the wavelength of the radiation. For example, certain computer forensic test procedures of electronic systems that require an environment free of electromagnetic interference can be carried out within a screened room. These rooms are spaces that are completely enclosed by one or more layers of a fine metal mesh or perforated sheet metal. The metal layers are grounded to dissipate any electric currents generated from external or internal electromagnetic fields, and thus, they block a large amount of the electromagnetic interference.

Shielded room

An ideal Faraday Cage or a shielded room is a sort of a metal box without any openings. Naturally, we need some openings for entering the shielded room, allowing for cable duct, and openings for vent and cooled air, etc. These aspects of a Faraday Cage relate to the cage's attenuation—which refers to the reduction in strength of an EMP wave as it attempts to enter the cage.

Shielded rooms are constructed in two optional methods in order to function as a Faraday Cage:

- A modular room with prefabricated 1-2mm steel plates which are collected and assembled on site with EMP-gaskets between all elements. This type gives very high attenuation and shielding effectiveness. It is also the most expensive option.

- "Thin plate" construction; on-site built shield with 26-gauge steel plates covering all room surfaces. This can be constructed on a DIY basis and gives a fairly high shielding effectiveness.

Both types of construction comply with most common regulatory attenuation requirements for civilian purposes. The shield itself must be constructed of an electric conductive material. Typically, thin galvanized steel plates are used, but in some cases, other metals like copper or brass foil are suitable. You can purchase 26-gauge steel sheets from your local steel fabricator or metal roof supplier.

Doors and Entryways

Doors in this type of shielded room are specially designed with high EMP attenuation performance. The door frame and leaf have a special EMP gasket for sufficient coupling and good sealing effect. An EMP proof door is expensive. There are DIY alternatives, but the cost of the door will be one of the biggest expenses of your shielded room.

There are two different types of such doors;

- High performance, EMP shielding door with knife frame and copper finger gasket. They cost thousands of dollars.

- A slightly less robust door designed like the lid of a Faraday Cage.

Option one is a professionally designed *shielding door* filled with special shielding materials to protect devices and human beings from invisible radioactive rays, electromagnetic waves, and microwaves. Depending on the purpose or use, the shielding door is categorized into *radiation shielding doors* which are installed in X-ray rooms, nuclear medicine rooms, Radioactive Isotope laboratories, or the radioactivity control rooms of industrial facilities, and *electromagnetic wave shielding doors* which are installed at magnetic wave shielding compartments, protecting medical instruments in hospitals or MRI rooms.

The electromagnetic wave shielded door protects a particular space against Radio Frequency or Conducted Noise which occurs due to unnecessary electromagnetic waves and hinders strong electromagnetic waves generated from an EMP. The conventional purpose of an electromagnetic wave shielded door is to protect devices at hospitals or laboratories from electromagnetic waves. They also are designed to withstand a high-altitude EMP attack.

Option two is to use a solid, pre-hung and fire-rated steel door with a steel welded frame. These can be purchased at any home improvement store for less than a thousand dollars. Cracks or openings should be filled with an EMP gasket and for added protection, the door frame and door handles should be sealed with aluminum foil tape when not in use.

We suggest a metal knit EMP shielding gasket which consists of a layer of knitted electrically conductive metal wires over a low-closure-force rubber or elastomer core. For heavy duty applications like an EMP, or for high temperature fire-proofing, the gasket is sometimes combined with an environmental seal.

These knitted wire mesh gaskets, available online, provide a cost-effective solution to high-shielding performance from an EMP. If you choose the all-metal knitted mesh or knitted metal mesh over an elastomer core, the door can be opened and closed frequently, as the gasket will allow recovery after compression. When combined with the pre-hung all steel entry door, you have a single entry system for roughly $1,200.

Single Entry Cabling and Ductwork

All cabling and ductwork for a cooling system is usually fed through the walls of the shielded room in one cable duct called the *Single Entry*. By reducing the number of cable entries to one, you can minimize the potential for low-frequency or high-frequency intrusion.

There are two types of Single Entry Cabling and Ductwork:

- A honeycomb shielding vent panel can be directly welded to your shielded steel walls. These are available online for under $200.

- Cable glands with mesh tube sealing; mounted directly on the shield wall. There are two types with different performances: a military grade that is outside of most budgets, and an industrial electromagnetic compatibility, or EMC glands. A single entry EMC gland plate is available online for around $200.

The EMP shielding vent panels consist of either a rectangular or a circular frame with a honeycomb structure inside. The honeycomb vent is series of hexagonal "tubes" that acts as a waveguide, guiding electromagnetic waves in/out of the shielded room and blocking the airflow. The airflow is led nearly unobstructed through the honeycomb while the electromagnetic pulses are stopped effectively.

CHAPTER TWENTY-TWO
SHIELDED CABLES, CABINETS AND ACCESSORIES

Electrical cables

As discussed in the prior chapter, all electric cables must be shielded when installed through a shielded room. This is an absolute requirement. Cables and wires act as an antenna during a geomagnetic storm event. Unshielded cables penetrating the shield will act as unwanted antennas and destroy the shield's effectiveness. Poorly shielded cables will cause serious leakages and damages of the internal installed equipment in the shielded room in the event of a HEMP.

Be aware that some high quality, but less recommended cables are available . Some manufacturers advertise and promote their shielded cables as *EMC*, without disclosing that some of these are not recommended for EMP protection. Quad-dense, braid/mesh shield or a mesh/foil shield is highly recommended, such as this cabling:

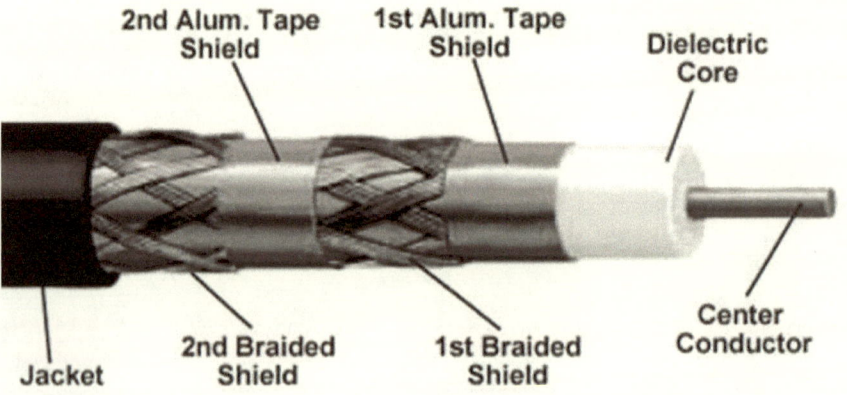

Shielded telephone wire is also suggested:

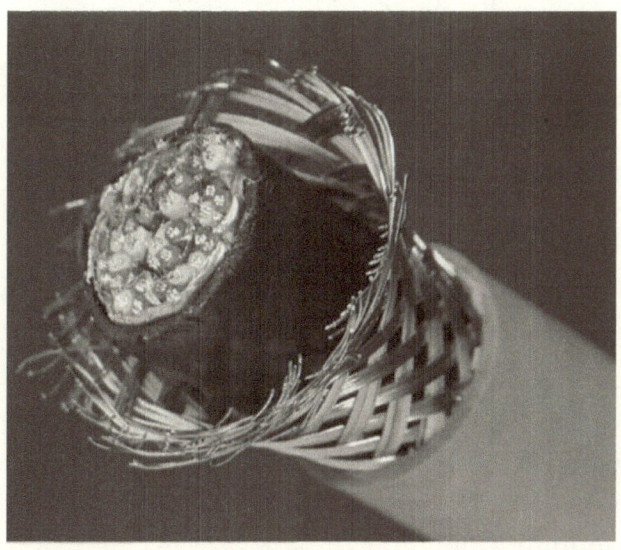

Finally, here is an example of shielded electrical wire:

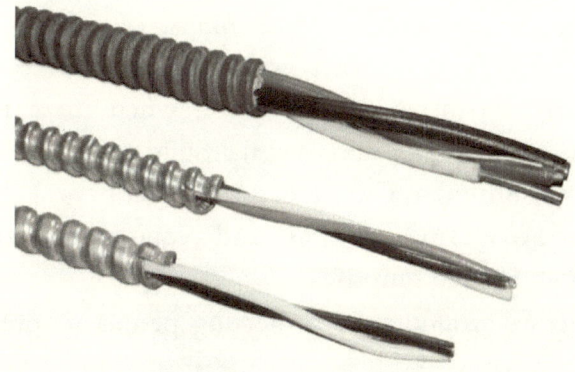

Shielded Racks/Cabinets

Shielded racks and cabinets can be constructed as Faraday Cages. There are two different types:

- Rugged, high-performance steel shelves with knife/copper EMP-gaskets in the door. Primarily used in industrial settings, this type is supplied with cable filters (power and telecom), in addition to the standard equipment like a small Single Entry, honeycombs and fans for vented air.

- Semi-rugged, high-performance steel racks with a simpler (less dense) mesh EMP-gasket in the door leaf. Like the above type, this is also typically equipped with honeycomb vents or a mesh door. However, this type is less costly.

Manufactured EMP-racks are expensive, but affordable compared with a professionally-installed shielded room. Assembly of cabinets is of course much easier and less expensive than the design/build of shielded rooms. An affordable alternative is to follow the instructions for creating a shielded room, but on a smaller scale—closet size.

Steel Shipping Container

An EMP-proof shipping container or shelter is a bigger Faraday Cage; steel box; built with approx. 3-5mm thick steel plates. Such containers are normally equipped with a shielded door, air vents with honeycomb, a Single Entry, cable filters, etc. The shielding effectiveness is very high; often equal to shielded rooms. This solution is fairly expensive, but effective, when there is lack of in-house space. The key is creating a seal around the entry door.

Grounding of Shielded Cabinets and Containers

Grounding of electric systems and equipment has several meanings, definitions and purposes:

- Protective grounding | protecting people to prevent user contact with dangerous voltage if electrical insulation fails.

- Functional grounding | usually the neutral in an electrical power supply system. For EMP shielded rooms and cabinets, the grounding "network" is essential for obtaining good shielding effectiveness. The shielding cabinets main purposes; EMP absorption and reflection, are dependent on a correctly grounded shield.

Since the shielding systems of a cabinet or shipping container may involve human contact, it is recommended to conduct and drain possible unwanted currents to a grounding source. Normally, the shield is connected with a massive grounding cable connected to the main earthing bar in the building and to the grounding rod outside. Correct grounding shall provide equal protection on the outside and inside of the shielded cabinet. It further avoids risk of electrocution by human contact.

Operation and Preventive Maintenance

The shielded enclosures and cabinets have to be regularly maintained to ensure specified shielding effectiveness. Typical maintenance activities are:

- General inspection and eventual repair of holes, slots, and other irregular openings in the enclosure

- Cleaning, lubrication, and greasing of EMP-gaskets

- Checking for possible EMP-gasket damages

- Door lock gear inspection and adjusting

- Air vents (honeycombs) dusting and vacuum cleaning

- Single Entry frame and modules inspection

- Filter inspection and bolt tightening

- Grounding and bonding cables inspection and tightening bolts, cable lugs, etc.

Mountain Plants/Underground Bunkers

Vulnerable electronic equipment could be adequately protected even without extra shielding in a Faraday Cage, if it is placed deep enough inside in a mountain plant or underground bunker. The shielding effectiveness is dependent on some important preconditions related to:

- Rock and soil environment depth and thickness

- Rock and soil type; i.e. the ground conductivity

- Cables from outside into the mountain or underground bunker; types, length, etc.

A note about construction, knowledge and competence

Construction and completion of shielded rooms is typically a process involving several parties like consultants, suppliers, installer companies, and dedicated consultants for a final test and control measurements. Common for all of these parties is a demand of sufficient competence, knowledge, and experience to secure high-quality performance and shielding effectiveness. If you are undertaking the construction of a shielded room, cost may or may not be a factor. These projects can be undertaken by anyone with a basic knowledge of construction, but testing is important after completion. At the very least, hire a competent professional to conduct the requisite testing.

Verification, test and measurements

After design, construction, and completion of a shielded room or installation of a cabinet, it is vital to check that the shield itself has obtained the designed and required shielding effectiveness. This is normally done in two steps; first, a careful visual inspection, followed by a set of tests and control measurements.

It is recommended to test a shielded room in two steps; first time after completion of the room construction, and finally after full installation of technical equipment with cabling, racks etc. The first step, will validate if the shield continuity is maintained and constructed correctly without holes, gaps, etc. The final step, will reveal wrong or poor installation of cables and tubes into the Single Entry, incorrect fixing or installation of equipment on walls, roof, etc.

After an EMP event is not the time to call an expert.

CHAPTER TWENTY-THREE
CONTENTS OF YOUR FARADAY CAGE

The Faraday Cage is an excellent solution, assuming that you aren't using the equipment when the event occurs. Following the prepper rule of redundancy—*three is two, two is one, one is none*—it is important to have one item of electronics for everyday use, and another secured in your Faraday Cage. Identify anything you may need after the grid-down event and keep it stored at all times.

Electronics to put in the Faraday Cage

First, you have to consider the size of the Faraday Cage. Again, applying the prepper rule of redundancy, have multiple cages with backups of certain electronic devices, especially medical ones. You should think about small electronics without which your life would be more difficult. Here are just a few examples:

- Hearing aid
- Electronic Blood Pressure machine, thermometer, defibrillator, blood sugar tester
- Solar powered radio, a crank radio, and a CB radio
- Two-way communications, HAM radio, including a smart phone
- Trail Cameras
- Laptop computer
- Computer Tablet loaded with preparedness related pdfs and survival guides
- LED flashlight with batteries

- Standard battery charger with rechargeable batteries

- Electronic Water Tester

- Handheld GPS and a GPS watch

- Buy an external hard disk with enough space to put all your computer back-ups on it and put it in the cage

- Laser Rangefinder

- Solar array equipment, charge controllers, wiring, etc.

- A radiation detector that will be very useful to check the radiation level after the EMP.

The list is not exclusive, and can go on according to how much space you've got. You can always make more than one Faraday Cage to store everything you might need. Inventory and label each Faraday Cage, so you don't have to break the outer seal unnecessarily.

Let's reiterate the importance of this chapter. Keep your essential electronics stored at all times. While we may receive advanced notice of a minimum of twelve hours for a geomagnetic storm, the rogue actors who threaten our nation daily with an EMP attack will not send a warning. Acquire the critical electronics necessary to survive in a post-TEOTWAWKI world, secure them in a Faraday Cage, and leave them there!

Because you never know when the day before, is the day before.

PART EIGHT
PREPARING FOR AN EMP ATTACK

Chapter Twenty-Four
Effects of an EMP on Vehicles

This is probably the single most prevalent topic of conversation when the effects of an electromagnetic pulse are discussed.

First, let's establish a few given facts. We have been unable to find any credible resource which has conducted testing on the effects of an EMP on a vehicle other than the use of the EMP cannon by law enforcement to disable a vehicle. When the high-altitude nuclear testing took place in the 1950's and early 1960's, automobiles did not have the extensive wiring and electronics of today's models.

Next, it is unlikely that a geomagnetic storm would harm an automobile's electronics because the E3 component of the electromagnetic pulse is not strong enough to cause damage to the wiring. A solar storm may impact the ability to obtain fuel.

The EMP Commission did conduct some testing on vehicles in 2002 and older models, but the electromagnetic pulse generated did not simulate the strength and power of a HEMP. Another caveat to the report of the EMP Commission is that their testing was limited due to funding. Vehicles used in these experiments were exposed to gradually increasing levels of electromagnetic pulse energy, up to the point where they began to show some kind of damage or malfunction. In order to save the vehicles from being excessively damaged, tests were halted immediately after a car or truck began to indicate some kind of dysfunction.

Here is an excerpt from the EMP Commission Critical National Infrastructures Report:

Automobiles

The potential EMP vulnerability of automobiles derives from the use of built-in electronics that support multiple automotive functions. Electronic components were first introduced into automobiles in the late 1960s. As time passed and electronics technologies evolved, electronic applications in automobiles proliferated. Modern automobiles have as many as 100 microprocessors that control virtually all functions. While electronic applications have proliferated within automobiles, so too have application standards and electromagnetic interference and electromagnetic compatibility (EMI/EMC) practices. Thus, while it might be expected that increased EMP vulnerability would accompany the proliferated electronics applications, this trend, at least in part, is mitigated by the increased application of EMI/EMC practices.

We tested a sample of 37 cars in an EMP simulation laboratory, with automobile vintages ranging from 1986 through 2002. Automobiles of these vintages include extensive electronics and represent a significant fraction of automobiles on the road today. The testing was conducted by exposing running and nonrunning automobiles to sequentially increasing EMP field intensities. If anomalous response (either temporary or permanent) was observed, the testing of that particular automobile was stopped. If no anomalous response was observed, the testing was continued up to the field intensity limits of the simulation capability (approximately 50 kV/m).

Automobiles were subjected to EMP environments under both engine turned off and engine turned on conditions. No effects were subsequently observed in those automobiles that were not turned on during EMP exposure. The most serious effect observed on running automobiles was that the motors in three cars stopped at field strengths of approximately 30 kV/m or above. In an actual EMP exposure, these vehicles would glide to a stop and require the driver to restart them. Electronics in the dashboard of one automobile were damaged and required repair. Other effects were relatively minor. Twenty-five automobiles exhibited malfunctions that could be considered only a nuisance (e.g., blinking dashboard lights) and did not require driver intervention to correct. Eight of the 37 cars tested did not exhibit any anomalous response.

Based on these test results, we expect few automobile effects at EMP field levels below 25 kV/m. Approximately 10 percent or more of the automobiles exposed to higher field levels may experience serious EMP effects, including engine stall, that require driver intervention to correct. We further expect that at least two out of three automobiles on the road will manifest some nuisance response at these higher field levels. The serious malfunctions could trigger car crashes on U.S. highways; the nuisance malfunctions could exacerbate this condition. The ultimate result of automobile EMP exposure could be triggered crashes that damage many more vehicles than are damaged by the EMP, the consequent loss of life, and multiple injuries.

Trucks

As is the case for automobiles, the potential EMP vulnerability of trucks derives from the trend toward increasing use of electronics. We assessed the EMP vulnerability of trucks using an approach identical to that used for automobiles. Eighteen running and nonrunning trucks were exposed to simulated EMP in a laboratory. The intensity of the EMP fields was increased until either anomalous response was observed or simulator limits were reached. The trucks ranged from gasoline-powered pickup trucks to large diesel-powered tractors. Truck vintages ranged from 1991 to 2003.

Of the trucks that were not running during EMP exposure, none were subsequently affected during our test. Thirteen of the 18 trucks exhibited a response while running. Most seriously, three of the truck motors stopped. Two could be restarted immediately, but one required towing to a garage for repair. The other 10 trucks that responded exhibited relatively minor temporary responses that did not require driver intervention to correct. Five of the 18 trucks tested did not exhibit any anomalous response up to field strengths of approximately 50 kV/m.

Based on these test results, we expect few truck effects at EMP field levels below approximately 12 kV/m. At higher field levels, 70 percent or more of the trucks on the road will manifest some anomalous response following EMP exposure. Approximately 15 percent or more of the trucks will experience engine stall, sometimes with permanent damage that the driver cannot correct. Similar to the case for automobiles, the EMP impact on trucks could trigger vehicle crashes on U.S. highways. As a result, many more vehicles could be damaged than those damaged directly by EMP exposure.

The best advice one can follow is to purchase a vehicle older than 1970, generally considered to be the pre-electronics age in the development of automobiles. Buy and store in a Faraday Cage ignition parts for your vehicle, including, but not limited to, an extra set of battery cables, a distributor, points, a condenser, starter motor, fuses, and spark plugs. Consider purchasing snap-on ferrite cores which act as a shield for electronic wiring of all types.

CHAPTER TWENTY-FIVE
IT'S TIME TO GET READY FOR THE COMING EMP ATTACK

Preparation, not panic, is the best way to face the threat of a grid-down collapse event.

The threats we face are many. At FreedomPreppers.com, Americans are urged to prepare for a worst-case scenario. If nothing happens, you've lost nothing. For the United States, short of nuclear annihilation, the worst-case scenario is an extended grid-down scenario.

The way you can protect yourself isn't very high-tech. In fact, you're going to be better off going low-tech.

Where do you begin in formulating a Preparedness Plan? An entire preparedness guide, hundreds of pages long, may still not adequately cover the elements of a comprehensive preparedness plan. The numerous disaster preparedness guides, blogs, and professional videos are all excellent resources. But where does one start?

Essentially, it all boils down to:

Beans, Band-Aids & Bullets

Well, of course, there is much more to developing a preparedness plan than the *big three*, but all preparedness experts know that these are the basics. Many preppers are well organized and rely heavily upon checklists. We urge you to review Appendix B which provides a summary as well as a link to a free pdf download of an extensive preparedness checklist. Preppers constantly update their checklists to ensure that they didn't overlook anything. You can as well.

As you review the following, keep in mind a few basic principles when preparing your plan.

The survival rule of threes: You can only live three minutes without air; three hours without shelter in extreme conditions; three days without water; and three weeks without food. This will help you prioritize your preps for a post-collapse survival situation.

The prepper rule of redundancy: Three is two, two is one, and one is none. When your prepper supplies run out, you can't drive down to Wal-Mart and restock.

Building your prepper supplies to an acceptable level for long-term survival requires baby steps. Thus, survival planning starts with the perfect trinity of prepping—*beans, band-aids and bullets*. Clearly, an oversimplification of what a preparedness plan entails, but it is a pretty good reflection of what you need have covered. This is a well-known expression within the prepper community, as it outlines the essentials that you will need in the event of TEOTWAWKI—the end of the world as we know it.

To summarize, *Beans* will include your prepper supplies, the items in your prepper pantry and water. *Band-aids* will refer to all things medical. *Bullets* will represent the weapons and ammunition necessary to protect yourself, your family and your preps.

Beans – Your Prepper Pantry

What is in your prepper pantry? Right now, take an honest assessment. How many days could your family survive on what's in your house right now? Most American households have less than seven days of food on hand.

Building a prepper pantry is one of those lifelines that take both time and planning to make it fully functional. Ideally, you want to store shelf-stable foods that your family normally consumes, as well as foods that serve multiple purposes. Stocking your prepper pantry should involve a combination of ready-to eat-food and beverages to last your family many months, plus long term food storage for a year or more.

Overall, your prepper pantry should reflect an abundance of the foods that you eat on a regular basis. Utilize a first in, first out rotation. This is a mistake many new preppers make. They buy food they don't eat on a regular basis. Instead, store your favorite foods that have a long shelf-life, that don't require refrigeration after opening, and that are easy to cook off the grid.

Our suggested preparedness plan includes non-perishable foods on our shelves to last us one year. Then we have canned vegetables, fruit, and meats created throughout the year. Finally, dried goods such as beans, rice, pasta, and oatmeal are stored utilizing Mylar Bags and desiccant packs (this technique is discussed in depth on the Freedom Preppers website) which can last for up to twenty years.

The following foods are all popular food staples that should be considered as "must haves" for your Prepper Pantry. The advantages to storing these items are that they encompass all of the key consideration points listed above. Best of all, these items are very affordable and extremely versatile, making them worthy of being on your storage shelves for extended emergencies. You'll find most of these items in your pantry already. Try to increase the quantity each week and place them into a rotation. Use this list as a starting point on beginning or extending your Prepper Pantry. Always keep your family's food preferences and dietary needs in mind when investing in your food supply. This list is very basic, but a good start. The checklist in Appendix B is helpful as well.

- Dried legumes such as beans, lentils, and peas

- Rice, lots of rice

- Pasta and sauces

- Oatmeal, Cream of Wheat, and cereals

- Canned meat, fish, soups, fruits, and vegetables

- Peanut Butter

- Packaged Meals (macaroni and cheese, hamburger helper, Ramen noodles

- Seasonings and cooking oils

- Flour, salt, sugar, corn meal, and powdered cheeses

- Powdered drinks like milk, Tang and Gatorade; Tea Bags

Here are some additional considerations.

Food – If you would like to start storing food, there are some things to think about. How long will the food last? Is this something that you and your family will realistically eat? Will the food survive if there is a disaster and no electricity? How will you cook the food that you have stored? The amount of food stored ultimately depends on the person that is storing it. But, keep in mind that you need to have enough food for the amount of time a foreseen disaster will last. If you are just preparing for a short term disaster, then maybe only a few days to a week of food is necessary. If your preparations need to last after a catastrophic collapse of society or a grid-down event, you may want to have a few months to multiple years of food stockpiled. Also, you may want to raise your own livestock and have a fruit and vegetable garden. Hunting and fishing are also a great way to supplement your food stores. Just a note, all of the grocery stores combined in one city, usually only have about three-days-worth of food for the entire city. This is known as *just-in-time inventory*, and most stores' shelves will be empty within hours when a collapse event becomes apparent.

Heirloom Seeds – While technically not food yet, the ability to grow your own food will be critical to sustain yourself after your food supplies run out. Besides, before the SHTF, *growing your own food was like printing your own money*. And, it's good practice.

Water – FEMA claims that each adult needs one gallon of water per person per day. This is wholly inadequate. While this quantity may keep you hydrated, it will not be sufficient to maintain your location. When there is no water coming out of the sink, where will you find fresh, clean water? You may want to keep water stockpiled as well. There are a couple options for this.

The basic principles revolve around *water catchment, purification, and storage*. Again, water management is a subject for an entire book. But consider this. In third world countries, dysentery is one of the major causes of death. In a grid-down scenario caused by an EMP, or otherwise, America will be set back into the nineteenth century from a technology standpoint. Drinking unclean water can kill you.

There are options. You can keep water bottles or gallon containers full. There are also water tanks that come in various sizes anywhere from under a hundred gallons up to thousands of gallons. If you are lucky enough to be near a river or lake, this may be a good source of water. There are many types and sizes of water filters that don't need electricity and make even the worst water safe to drink. There are also tablets that can be placed in water to purify it. A well would also be a fantastic water source, but can be quite pricey to build. Ultimately, there are many options, but it is a good idea to know about the natural water sources in your area.

Pets – Finally, please do not forget your pets. They are family too and dogs, in particular, may be a useful asset in your home's defenses.

Bandaids – Your Armageddon Medicine Cabinet

After a collapse event, you will probably not have ready access to a dentist or doctor, much less a hospital. Available treatment will be scarce and required medicines even scarcer. When you become injured or sick, help will not be on the way. You will become the primary care physician for your prepper group.

Survival Medicine requires you to have a substantial preppers First Aid Kit, complete with over-the-counter and pharmacy medications. You will need to gain the knowledge necessary to diagnose and treat a variety of illnesses and injuries, including dental care.

Preventative Medicine – Though not a conventional aspect of beans, bullets, and band-aids, staying in shape and being healthy is one of the best ways to prevent problems after any collapse event. When we are healthy, we are able to work harder and more efficiently. Being healthy and in shape can also promote productivity. Some of the ways to prepare for an end of the world scenario are to eat right, exercise regularly, and keep an active lifestyle. Knowledge of minor medical procedures is also a great way to prepare.

Prescription Medications – If you need a certain prescription to maintain a productive lifestyle, make sure to have a surplus of them on hand. There are some doctors that will give extra prescriptions for the purpose of preparing and stockpiling, so the beans, bullets and bandaids theory suggests asking and explaining your situation to your physician. Additionally, there are some medicines that should be kept on hand; antibiotics are an important one. We suggest stockpiling fish antibiotics, as they are some of the most useful to treat infections. But don't forget the many over-the-counter medicines that are used regularly. These can include aspirin, allergy medicines, cold or flu remedies, diarrhea medicines, stool softeners, and many more. Medical supplies such as those found in a first aid or trauma kit are very important. For instance, how will you dress a wound or set a broken bone? It is good to have band aids, bandages, braces, splints, and thermometers on hand. The more you know and have, increases the chances of surviving.

Hygiene – Maintaining personal hygiene and sanitation after the collapse event is critical. Ingesting bacteria may kill you without access to proper medical care. Consider this: How many rolls of toilet paper does your family use a day? What will you use as an alternative when you run out? Where do you plan to poop when the SHTF? Got the picture?

Prepping for hygiene may be as simple as obtaining multiples of everyday household items. Savvy preppers know they need to stockpile a supply of food and water but hygiene products are essential to decrease the spread of disease and illness. It's also helps you maintain a sense of normalcy.

In a post-SHTF world, sanitation and hygiene will be important to keep yourself and your family healthy. Running water may no longer be an option or a healthy choice, and you need to know how to practice good hygiene, proper sanitation and keep your environment healthy. These are all very important considerations in a SHTF situation. Due to a lack of available medical facilities or treatment, health and disease prevention are going to be more important and more difficult to treat than ever after TEOTWAWKI.

Sanitation items are easy to gather. You may prefer a pre-assembled emergency kit which already contains necessary items for grooming and sanitation. Because many kit items are sold as a unit, you may find that purchasing a kit is an inexpensive and convenient way to prepare all that you'll need during an emergency. Another option may be to assemble your own emergency kit, so you can choose brands or items your family is accustomed to using. Often, you can purchase your favorite brand of soap, toothpaste, shampoo, toilet paper, deodorant, and other items in bulk or extra-saving packages, so you can afford to set some aside for your emergency kit.

The best advice here is to pay attention to what you use every day. From the moment you awake, until you fall asleep. Do you have three to twelve months of each item that you use? Perform this task for a week and then imagine if the grid collapsed, and store shelves were empty. How would you perform that particular task?

Here are some items to consider:

Toilet Paper – When it comes to emergencies, any kind of toilet paper is a luxury. By preparing ahead of time, you can ensure that you don't experience the unneeded discomfort by a lack of toilet paper. Further, it is common for those in emergency situations to develop stress and diet related stomach problems that can intensify your sanitation difficulties.

Toothbrush + Oral Hygiene – People with sensitive teeth may want to store their preferred brand of toothbrush in their emergency kit. It is probably a wise idea to store several toothbrushes to give away to someone who neglected to store one. It may also have another useful purpose; such as cleaning or scrubbing.

Toothpaste, Mouthwash, and Breath Fresheners – Emergencies present stressful situations where human communication is crucial. Sometimes, water is scarce or unavailable which causes dryness in your mouth. A breath freshener may be a nice addition to your preparedness supplies.

Feminine Hygiene Products – It is important to be prepared in all areas. These items are definitely important to have available in any emergency situation.

Deodorant – With several choices of deodorants including hypo-allergenic, made-for-a-woman brands, gelled, etc., you may want to decide ahead of time what you'll need during an emergency.

Air fresheners or deodorants may also increase your level of comfort during an emergency.

Hair Supplies – Shampoo, conditioner, hairspray, combs, brushes, and other items may not be necessary for survival, but they can help make an emergency situation more comfortable and clean. Be sure to store smaller sanitation items in your emergency kit, but be aware that you can overstuff your emergency kit. If it is too heavy, you may not be able to leave with it during an emergency.

Medications for diarrhea, constipation, headaches, allergy and other minor conditions should also be included in kits for added comfort.

Laundry Detergent and Soap – During some emergencies, you may be required to evacuate the area or may be stranded in some remote area. Because you won't have lots of clothing, you will want detergent to clean your clothes and soap for bathing and for washing utensils.

Hand sanitizers are essential to keep in your kit or bug-out bag as well.

Bathing – You can prevent illness by washing your hands often; before eating, after using the bathroom, after you change a diaper, and any other time you may need to freshen up. Because water is such a precious commodity during an emergency, you should remember to use purified drinking water first for drinking, cooking, washing dishes and then for other purposes. Be organized and choose a designated bathing area. If you wash in a river or stream, use biodegradable soap and always be aware of others who may be down stream. With a little soap, you can also wash yourself in the rain. Other washing alternatives include moist towelettes, a spray bottle, sanitizing lotions, or a wet washcloth. Be sure to wear shoes to prevent parasitic infections and to protect you from cuts and puncture wounds that can easily become infected.

Sanitation Area – Choosing the right location for your sanitation needs is as important as staying clean. Your waste place must be located downhill from any usable water source. It should also be a few hundred feet from any river, stream, or lake. It also helps to have your waste place downwind from your living area, and yet not too far from your camp that the distance discourages people from using it.

Luggable Loo – With a little preparation, you can have a decent emergency toilet. If you have a five-gallon plastic bucket lined with a heavy-duty garbage bag, you have a toilet. Don't forget to add deodorized cat litter to assist with the odor. Make sure you have a lid to cover it. A plastic toilet seat can be purchased to fit on the bucket for a more comfortable seat. If you don't have an extra plastic bucket available, you can make a latrine by digging a long trench approximately one-foot wide and twelve to eighteen inches deep and cover as you go. When you dig too deep a latrine, it can slow the bacterial breakdown process. The long latrine approach is appropriate for large groups camping in one spot for a long period.

Getting Rid of Refuse – If you cannot dispose of refuse properly, you should always bury biodegradable garbage and human waste to avoid the spread of disease by rats and insects. Dig a pit twelve to eighteen inches deep and at least fifty feet, but preferably two hundred feet downhill and away from any well, spring, or water supply. Fill the pit with the refuse and cover with dirt. For back-country hikers, packing out all solid waste is always appropriate, and some authorities at high-use rivers usually require this process. You can make a seat for your latrine by laying logs across the hole, leaving an area open for you to use. After use, cover the waste with small amounts of dirt to decrease the odor. A covered toilet reduces more of the odor than an open one. Make a toilet cover with wood or a large leaf. If the odor becomes unbearable, fill in the latrine completely with dirt and dig a new one. Build a new seat and burn the old wood that you used for the last toilet.

Keeping Food Sanitary – All food scraps should be either burned or buried in a pit far from your living area to keep bears and other wild animals away from you. Keep all of your food covered and off the ground. You may keep your food in a tree, but be sure that tree-dwelling creatures can't get into it. Replace all lids on water bottles and other containers immediately after use. Do not wash your dishes in the area where you get your drinking water supply. Instead, wash your dishes away from a stream. Use clean plates or eat out of the original food containers to prevent the spread of germs. Wash and peel all fruits and vegetables before eating. Prepare only as much as will be eaten at each meal.

Bullets – Your SHTF Defense Tools
Bottom Line: If you can't defend it, it isn't yours.

Conceptually, preparation without security is meaningless. It doesn't matter if you hate guns. Perhaps your political or religious beliefs prevent you from committing acts of violence, or self-defense. After TEOTWAWKI, the world will become a brutal place. The world we live in will not be unicorns and rainbows. Unless you are prepared to give up your preps, or even your life, all preppers need a security plan.

Actual security countermeasures can be quite complex, but they generally conform to the five principles of prepper security. A security plan involves the five D's:

Deter ~ Deny ~ Detect ~ Delay ~ Defend

The first *D* is *deter*. The first goal is to deter an attack by giving the appearance of a robust security program and substantial physical barriers. Deterrence also comes from aggressive defensive positioning. Countermeasures include an alert security force, vehicle checkpoints & searches, guard towers, visible weapons positions, lighting, and armed patrols pushing out from the immediate perimeter.

The second principle is to *deny* access through physical barriers and security forces. Types of physical barriers include trenches, fences, concertina wire, razor ribbon, Hesco baskets, and concrete barriers. In the absence of construction resources, security guard forces can be positioned to deny access. However, the fewer physical barriers in place, the greater the security forces required to deny access into your perimeter.

The third *D* is *detect*. Early detection of an attempted intrusion or breach of your perimeter is critical to an effective defensive response. Detection is best achieved through open ground, cleared area, and alert security personnel. Assuming a grid-down scenario, this can be augmented with guard dogs, trip flares, battery operated alarm systems, and other noise or light generating devices.

The fourth principle is to *delay* your aggressor. When your physical barriers or security forces cannot stop an attack, they should at least be positioned to delay the approach. Additional barriers allow your security forces the time to regroup, reassess and reengage the approaching attack. An effective delaying tactic will allow for reinforcements of your perimeter security forces.

The fifth *D* is *defend*, or as some might say—*destroy*. To put it bluntly, *kill or be killed*. Without rule of law—WROL—the Rules of Engagement with your adversaries will change. Make no mistake, *defend*, or the concept of *self-defense*, will be defined differently after a collapse event. The best defense is to destroy your enemy with whatever weapons are available to you. Otherwise, a sixth *D* results—*deceased*.

But, if you follow proper OPSEC, Operational Security, discussed at length below, you can minimize the number of threats that you face—especially if you follow disciplined OPSEC prior to the collapse event. Otherwise, you will face the sixth *D*.

Protection – Having a way to protect yourself and your family is very important during trying times, as people in desperate situations will take desperate measures. Guns are a very important part of protection and may be able to diffuse a situation where talking and negotiating do not resolve the situation. There are many different types of guns and many theories on which ones to own. Each type of weapon has different uses in a variety of situations. If your target is relatively close, a shotgun or pistol may be the best option. If your target is sixty yards or more away, a rifle is probably the best option. However, protection is not just limited to guns. Reusable and quiet weapons such as bows or knives are great to have because you constantly run the risk of depleting your bullet stockpile. Protection could also be in the form of a fence or barbed wire outside your home that deters thieves and other mischievous people.

Hunting- This also goes into the food category of beans, bullets and band-aids. In order to hunt efficiently and effectively, you need to know which hunting weapons to purchase and use. A .22 rifle would be much better for squirrel and varmint hunting than an AR-15. However, a .308 caliber rifle would be more effective for hunting deer or other big game animals. A bow may be better in any situation, as it is silent and will not arouse attention like a gun. Another great idea is the use of traps. These are reusable and are semi-passive ways of finding food. They can also protect your home from intruders. In the forest and plains areas, squirrels, elk, deer, birds, turkeys and water fowl are all great sources of protein.

Finally, a word about *operational security*—**OPSEC**. This brings us to another important axiom of prepping:

Tell No One About Your Preps!

The prepper's creed begins:

If you don't talk, no one will hear and if no one else hears, no one else will know.

Operational Security, or OPSEC, for Preppers is a discipline, a mindset. It is simply denying an adversary, present or future, vital information that could harm you or benefit them.

Prior to collapse, OPSEC involves curtailing your activities on social media or not bragging about your weapons cache.

As kids, we found comfort in our homes with our families, maybe hiding under the covers or with a favorite blanket. As we've grown up, our concerns may focus on job security, financial security and general home security. Now we are big boys and girls—preparing for TEOTWAWKI. Security takes on a whole new meaning when you have to fear armed marauders streaming down your driveway to take your preps, or worse. Your favorite blankie won't help you.

Once there is a life-changing collapse event, you may take comfort in knowing you're well prepped with all the beans, band-aids, and bullets that a well-prepared family could need. Well, guess what? Your failure to abide by OPSEC guidelines will quickly make you a target. There is a relatively simple SOP—standard operating procedure—for survival groups who've advanced to the highest level of preparedness. How can you avoid armed confrontations with the marauders? What should you do prior to the collapse event, in order to keep your preps hidden from the world?

Pre-Collapse: Getting Others to Prep

Getting other people to prep is far easier said than done. If it were easy to convince people to spend their hard-earned money on a possible bad future, then we'd all be prepared and there wouldn't be a fear of looting and raiding. But it isn't easy and those threats are real.

When first talking to someone about prepping, you need to understand your audience. This means that if you're talking to a hard-core outdoorsman, you can bring up far more *survival-esque* components to prepping, while a friend that is just talking about a natural disaster should be eased into it more.

Secondly, it's important to focus on the need to prep over the possible reasons. People don't like thinking about economic collapse or cyber warfare, so instead of hearing you talk about prepping, those people will instead argue the finer points of why those things can't happen. If you focus on the possibility of something making food, water, or essentials like toilet paper hard to get, it only makes sense to prepare for that possibility. Whatever the case, getting people on board by scaring them doesn't work, but getting them to understand their lives without the essentials, is a sure fire way to get them signed up.

Once you get friends and family on board with prepping for themselves, it's easier to talk with them and for everyone to help each other. There's something to be said for acting alone—*the lone wolf prepper*, but a little help will never hurt. If you make the determination to form a group, you can proceed with caution.

Pre-Collapse: Forming a prepper group

As preppers, you face a conundrum. Should you be part of a prepper group or should you be a lone wolf prepper? There are benefits and detriments to both options. Here are some considerations in forming a prepper group.

One of the first things a new prepper typically wants to do is reach out to other like-minded people in their area about prepping and try to form a prepper group. Unless there is an established and open group in the area, it's often very difficult to form a post-collapse team. Preppers are naturally cautious about discussing prepping with people that they don't already know. Unless the group is actively looking for new members, you might not even know about a group in your area.

If you are serious about prepping, then you have probably come to the realization that you will not be able to do everything yourself when SHTF. Just the day-to-day chores of collecting firewood, sanitation issues, cooking, food procurement, and cleaning without modern technology, will be overwhelming for a family, but when you have the added issue of providing your own security. You will quickly realize that you'll need help in maintaining security.

A prepper group is an association of people that have agreed to help each other out after a collapse event. The level of help depends on the scenario, the people involved, and the community. Some prepper groups encompass an entire small town or community. Typically, the residents intend to stay in their own homes, but agree to provide mutual security and aid on a community-wide scale. Because of their size, these types of groups are rare, and formed post-collapse.

The most common type of group is a loosely organized group of people, which may or may not live close to each other, but have general plans to provide mutual aid. They might meet together on a regular basis to discuss different scenarios, take classes together, and combine orders for bulk purchasing. Some are well-organized, while others just pay lip-service to the concept. A prepper group like this might be beneficial during the planning stage, but in an actual event, the distance between them will make mutual aid impossible.

The next prepper group is a collaboration of several like-minded individuals that have made a plan, practiced their plan, and have a mutually agreed upon location to execute that plan as a group. They live fairly close to each other, but instead of trying to stay in their various locations, recognize the importance of being together to provide strength in numbers. This is the best case scenario.

Putting together a prepper group does not mean that you must find a group of survivalists and band together. There are several things that you need to consider when deciding if someone is right for your group. Factors include:

1. What are they prepping for?
2. What skills or supplies do they bring to the table?

3. How many in their group and what is their relationship to each other?

4. How committed are they?

When we look at forming our prepping group, we have to consider if the people are like-minded, their skills, commitment, and who they will bring with them. Later, for recruiting purposes, we also need to consider how many people we will need, to accomplish what needs to be done

Recently, a Prepper in the Tampa, Florida area learned a hard lesson in choosing members for his preppers group. Many of the newest members had prior felonies, which prohibited them from owning or possessing firearms. Further, this Florida prepper engaged in questionable conduct; such as building pipe bombs and making veiled threats against law enforcement. When one of his new members of the group was arrested on unrelated charges, they turned snitch and wore a wire during the prepper's group meetings. The end result—the leader of the group is going to prison, while the snitch walks free.

The debate will always rage as to whether you should be a member of a preppers group or a lone wolf prepper. Regardless of how you define your prepper group, there are common issues when determining who to let your group. It is a private membership which should always practice OPSEC, due to the sensitive information that everyone in the group has access to. You need to give careful consideration to the people becoming part of your group. In general, this is not an easy topic, as there are no fast and simple rules. The average human being is a complex bag of emotions and logic, to which fields of science have been dedicated to understanding. Therefore, it is not surprising when the person you had thought to be a stable individual, turns out to be not much more than a basket-case.

Consider this. Choosing members of a preppers group is a lot like courting; you cannot really tell if they are right for you from just a few dates. Sure, we've all heard of love at first sight. However, given time, a person's true colors shine through. Being part of a group is not much different. There will be differences, arguments, heated debates, betrayals, and various other emotional conflicts. All of which need to be addressed, particularly, since this group is supposed to be like a second family to you.

One very important aspect to keep in mind is what will happen when someone stops being a group member. Though it may seem like many people would make a good group member, most will turn out to be incompatible with you and your group. Some people are very good at hiding who they really are, even after knowing someone for years. What has the newly-ejected member learned about you, your family, and your preparedness plan? They may get kicked out of the group or they may decide to leave voluntarily. Either way, this person becomes a security risk.

When looking at group preparedness, remember that a long-term crisis scenario will require large amounts of labor for survival. Therefore, unless you are creating a specific paramilitary team, no one should be automatically discounted because of any disabilities or shortcomings (such as having a lack of gear). Look at each prospective member on a case-by-case basis, weighing their strengths and weaknesses, while keeping in mind that everyone has something to contribute. Finding group members is a tedious process, but the gains accomplished by having a group of people you can depend on, are immeasurable.

Your survival may depend on it.

Post-collapse: How to Assimilate with your neighbors to form a group

These are all considerations of OPSEC for preppers that can be implemented prior to the collapse event. After TEOTWAWKI, when other factors like a grid-down scenario come into play, OPSEC becomes less technology oriented.

After collapse, OPSEC will require you to resist the urge to step up and be the new leader of any newly-formed survival group. One of the biggest mistakes preppers can make is to tell the wrong person or people about their preps. While helping people in a time of need, is one of the most selfless things you can do, if you're the only person prepared in your neighborhood and everyone comes looking to you for help, all of your pre-collapse OPSEC will be wasted, as desperate people attempt to take the things you've worked so hard to save. We believe that it is better to be safe, keep our preparedness plans to ourselves, than to be sorry.

While you don't want to tell the world about your plans, it's expected that you might want to share with close friends, family, and possibly trusted co-workers. To help you understand who you should tell and who you shouldn't, we've put together a few points.

Complete privacy is nearly impossible to keep, especially when you will surely need help with something at some point. It will be very difficult to survive on your own. The biggest reason to form a survival group, in our opinion, is to maintain security. After a collapse event, your world will become much smaller. Your neighborhood will become your universe. Focus on establishing a group of neighbors first, and then look outward for like-minded thinkers.

The goal is to survive, and if potential looters know what you have, that survival will be a big challenge. Within days if not hours of the collapse event, your neighbors will begin to gather together to seek information. You will have a decision to make. Step up and be the leader of the group, or stand back and observe. We are in favor of continuing your OPSEC practice after collapse, and avoiding a leadership role at first.

Here are the steps we recommend you take after a collapse event:

1. Take a day to gather information and assess the extent of the collapse. Observe your neighbors to gauge their reaction.

2. Maintain a heightened state of awareness. Every action and reaction of your neighbors should be observed, and not dismissed.

3. Be polite to everyone you deal with, but do so with confidence. You do not want to be perceived as weak.

4. Learn about the people around you from reliable sources. Immediately attempt to identify troublemakers.

5. Identify cliques within your neighborhood, and identify individuals or families to approach. You have to establish trust.

6. Initially, don't worry about ascertaining the level of other people's preps. Avoid suspicion by not being too inquisitive.

7. If a neighborhood meeting is called, determine who the organizers are. Typically, these individuals will be type A, overbearing temperaments.

8. Don't make waves. Better to remain quiet, than to argue. Your job is not to take control, or provide information.

9. Conceal your weapons, and do not discuss your preps, EVER.

In summary, focus on your immediate family. You shouldn't tell anyone else about your plans. This means, if you tell your parents that live outside your house (which of course you will), you will need to save supplies for them as well. If you tell your close friends, you will need food and water for them, too. If you tell anyone, they immediately become part of your plan. This is why the final step is getting those special people in your life to prep as well. This way, you now have a network of trusted preppers that can help one another now, and when times get tough. Once you have them all at your location, then you can begin to take a more active role in your neighborhood survival group. Your close-knit group of family and friends can defend your preps, in case there is an uprising amongst your neighbors.

So the big question is, *who should I tell about my prepping?* The answer is anyone that you feel comfortable surviving TEOTWAWKI with. If you want to house enough supplies for all of your neighbors to come and enjoy, tell them at your own risk. Even then, you run the risk of them telling their friends and so on, until you have a hundred people at your door looking for a handout. Help people with knowledge and never let on to the size of your prep or the weapons that you have. Getting to know your neighbors will be a big help. You will be able to determine who has the will and aptitude to survive a collapse event. After a collapse, cautiously approach those neighbors to form alliances, and encourage them to use their skills to help themselves and your group.

This is only a start to the concept of beans, bullets and band-aids. The one thing I haven't discussed yet is the importance of research and knowledge. If money is an issue, this is a great place to start. This necessary step to survival just happens to be free. There are many great books and tutorials online, or at local libraries, that will teach you anything from CPR to fishing and gardening at no cost. Now that you know about beans, bullets and bandaids, you can start preparing for any scenario you see fit.

John F. Kennedy once said *the time to repair the roof is when the sun is shining.* Because you never know when the day before—is the day before. Prepare for tomorrow.

Thanks for reading!

SIGN UP to Bobby Akart's mailing list to receive a **FREE** book in one of his other bestselling series. You'll also be one of the first to receive news about new releases in The Boston Brahmin Series and the Prepping for Tomorrow series. http://eepurl.com/bk7i_9

Visit Bobby Akart's website for informative blog entries on preparedness, writing and his latest contribution to the American Preppers Network.
www.BobbyAkart.com

Stop by the Boston Brahmin website to dig deeper into the history, characters, and real-life events that inspired the series.
www.TheBostonBrahmin.com

Visit the Freedom Preppers website to learn about all aspects of preparedness and the threats we face.

www.FreedomPreppers.com

READ about the threat our nation faces from a devastating cyber attack. CYBER WARFARE, part of the Prepping for Tomorrow series, achieved #1 bestseller rankings in eight genres on Amazon.

APPENDIX A
EXCERPT FROM THE LOYAL NINE

**The following is an excerpt from
Amazon Best-Selling Author Bobby Akart**

Chapter 25
February 8, 2016
Harvard Kennedy School of Government
Cambridge, Massachusetts

Sarge was late for class. A massive pileup on the Mass Turnpike, near the Beacon Park rail yard, forced him to drive the long way, via Beacon Hill and East Cambridge. Ordinarily, he would enjoy the change of scenery, but he had already been running late. He and Julia had a sleepover—devoid of much sleep.

He entered the classroom to a round of throat clearing, followed by sarcastic applause. He gathered his thoughts and brought up the first slide on the screen:

ALL EMPIRES COLLAPSE EVENTUALLY

He turned to the class and took a moment to gauge their reaction. *Let's see what they think about this topic.*

"Okay, guys, what do you think I mean by this?" asked Sarge.

A few hands shot up. Sarge pointed at a meek student in the back of the room. *Time to come out of your shell.*

"Mr. Lin, what say you?"

"Professor Sargent, I believe that in the history of mankind, every civilization ever formed has eventually disappeared or been replaced," said Lin.

"How does this come about, Mr. Lin?" asked Sarge.

"They either go broke or get their asses kicked," said Lin.

This elicited a round of laughter from his classmates. Sarge was also amused. *So much for Mr. Lin's shell.*

"Thank you, Mr. Lin, for that concise, articulate answer," Sarge chuckled. "All empires collapse eventually when they are defeated by a more powerful enemy or when their funding runs out."

"Ladies and Gentlemen, there have been no exceptions in the history of mankind. Empires are not typically the result of conscious thought. Empires form when a group of people is large enough and powerful enough to impose its will on others—or *kick their asses*," said Sarge with a nod and smile to Lin.

"But empires are expensive," continued Sarge. "Throughout history, how did the mighty empires of the world finance themselves?"

Sarge saw the hands pop up. He chose Miss Crepeau.

"To the victor go the spoils," she replied.

"Exactly. Thank you, Miss Crepeau," said Sarge. "In the early 1800s, this phrase was coined by a New York politician, but we have President Andrew Jackson to thank for the modern-day patronage system, which is so prevalent in our government today. President Jackson believed it was healthy to clear out the prior administration's workers and bring in fresh faces. This patronage policy resulted in many *Jacksonian Democrats*, his political supporters, being placed into important government positions."

Sarge allowed the playful banter between warring political factions in the class to settle down before interrupting.

"Before the Republicans point fingers, I will remind you—the Southern Democrats of the early nineteenth century are the political equivalent of today's Southern Republican base," said Sarge.

The class erupted in another round of political posturing.

"So," said Sarge, pausing to bring the class back to attention, "to Miss Crepeau's point, empires have historically financed their governments through force and theft. The great empires conquer their lesser opponents, take everything they have, and extort protection money out of the conquered citizens. This is how all of the great empires of the world were formed.

"Some might argue that the United States is different—and in some respects it is," said Sarge. "America was not formed by conquering another, less powerful opponent, although the Native Americans might disagree. The Founding Fathers sought independence from what they considered oppressive rule from Great Britain. But the formation of the great American empire, if you will, is only part of the equation."

Sarge brought up a new screen.

Who's going to pay for this new empire?

"Part two of the formation of a new empire involves financing its operations," said Sarge. "America didn't conquer another nation and plunder its wealth. The premise of the American Revolutionary War included a revolt against the implementation of taxes on the citizenry. Clearly, there wasn't a stomach for that. What did they do to pay for this new government?"

The young law student, Ocampo, eagerly raised his hand.

"Mr. Ocampo," said Sarge, "what do you think?"

"They fired up the printing presses, sir," said Ocampo.

"That's true to an extent," said Sarge. "The Constitution provided in Article One that the federal government had the sole power *to coin money and regulate the value thereof.* But the Constitution was devoid of reference to paper money. You see, the Founding Fathers had some experience with paper money. The Continental Congress, as Ocampo suggested, fired up the printing presses and financed the American Revolution with a newly minted currency — *continentals.* Unfortunately, although I would argue predictably, the *continentals* became worthless by the end of the war—to the point they were never spoken of again.

"It wasn't until the Civil War when the National Banking Act was passed that the paper dollar became the fully accepted currency of the land," said Sarge. "The United States adopted a gold standard, and its currency value became universally accepted. This leads us to one of the most important acts of participation by our country in global governance in its history—the Bretton Woods Conference."

Sarge changed the slide.

"After the conclusion of World War II, delegates from the forty-four Allied nations participated in the UN Financial and Monetary Conference in Bretton Woods, New Hampshire. This conference produced the International Monetary Fund and the World Bank," said Sarge. "At the time, the United States was the world's greatest economic power and had a lot of influence on the agreements reached. Study the history and background of the Bretton Woods system. This is a prime example of the impact of global governance." Sarge changed the slide again.

The Nixon Shock

"Welcome to the Nixon Shock, the mother of all government economic intervention," said Sarge. "In essence, among other things, President Nixon abandoned the gold standard and the United States dollar became strictly a fiat currency. This is when we fired up the printing presses, Mr. Ocampo, and we haven't stopped since.

"You see, America never grasped the whole concept of being an empire. We conquered, but we did not take anything like our predecessors. In fact, history will show that we lose money on every conquest. Typically, after destroying another country in battle, we then move in and pay to fix it back. We lose money every time," said Sarge, returning to a previous slide.

Who's going to pay for this?

"So how does a nation that conquers without obtaining the spoils of victory sustain itself?" asked Sarge. "They do it with debt. No other empire has ever tried to finance itself by borrowing from others. No other nation has ever tried to borrow its own currency; which it prints any time it chooses. As we have seen in recent years, if the burden of repaying this debt is too high, the Federal Reserve simply prints more dollars to satisfy its creditors. They call this Ponzi scheme *quantitative easing*. The United States government is paying its prior debt obligations by issuance of new debt obligations or the printing of new money out of thin air. There are people sitting in Federal Prison for this exact type of scheme.

"Today, our national debt, the amount we owe our creditors, is twenty trillion dollars. Every year, we add another one point two trillion to this total," said Sarge. "Many argue that this trend is unsustainable, which leads us back to our original premise." Sarge changed the slide back to the beginning. He had come full circle.

ALL EMPIRES COLLAPSE EVENTUALLY

"All empires collapse when they are defeated by a more vigorous empire, such as China, Russia or any of a number of rogue nations who possess nuclear capabilities," said Sarge. "Or empires collapse when their financing runs out. America has built up a tremendous amount of debt that is owed to countries that do not like us very much—like China and Russia.

"I want you to consider this. Should China and Russia elect to devalue our currency, resulting in our allies such as Germany and Japan becoming skittish about purchasing more of our debt, what would be the fate of the almighty dollar?" asked Sarge rhetorically. "If the United States cannot continue to finance itself via debt instruments, then it must tax its citizenry at an unprecedented rate. I submit to you that there isn't enough income or wealth in this country to cover the bill."

Sarge pointed to the screen.

"I will leave you with this. If all empires eventually collapse, does this premise also apply to the United States? If so, is this the beginning of the end?"

APPENDIX B
PREPAREDNESS CHECKLIST
PROVIDED BY WWW.FREEDOMPREPPERS.COM

FOR PREPPERS CHECKLIST
VISIT:
http://www.freedompreppers.com/preppers-checklist-free-pdf-download.htm

APPENDIX C
EMP COMMISSION REPORT, EXECUTIVE SUMMARY

April 2008
CRITICAL NATIONAL INFRASTRUCTURES

DUTIES OF COMMISSION

(a) Review of EMP Threat. The Commission shall assess:

(1) the nature and magnitude of potential high-altitude EMP threats to the United States from all potentially hostile states or non-state actors that have or could acquire nuclear weapons and ballistic missiles enabling them to perform a high-altitude EMP attack against the United States within the next 15 years;

(2) the vulnerability of United States military and especially civilian systems to an EMP attack, giving special attention to vulnerability of the civilian infrastructure as a matter of emergency preparedness;

(3) the capability of the United States to repair and recover from damage inflicted on United States military and civilian systems by an EMP attack; and

(4) the feasibility and cost of hardening select military and civilian systems against EMP attack.

(b) Recommendation. The Commission shall recommend any steps it believes should be taken by the United States to better protect its military and civilian systems from EMP attack.

The findings and recommendations presented in this report are the independent judgments of this Commission and should not be attributed to any other people or organizations. This report presents the unanimous views of the Commissioners.

ABSTRACT

Several potential adversaries have or can acquire the capability to attack the United States with a high-altitude nuclear weapon-generated electromagnetic pulse (EMP). A determined adversary can achieve an EMP attack capability without having a high level of sophistication.

EMP is one of a small number of threats that can hold our society at risk of catastrophic consequences. EMP will cover the wide geographic region within line of sight to the nuclear weapon. It has the capability to produce significant damage to critical infrastructures and thus to the very fabric of US society, as well as to the ability of the United States and Western nations to project influence and military power.

The common element that can produce such an impact from EMP is primarily electronics, so pervasive in all aspects of our society and military, coupled through critical infrastructures. Our vulnerability is increasing daily as our use of and dependence on electronics continues to grow. The impact of EMP is asymmetric in relation to potential protagonists who are not as dependent on modern electronics.

The current vulnerability of our critical infrastructures can both invite and reward attack if not corrected. Correction is feasible and well within the Nation's means and resources to accomplish.

OVERVIEW

EMP IS CAPABLE OF CAUSING CATASTROPHE FOR THE NATION

The high-altitude nuclear weapon-generated electromagnetic pulse (EMP) is one of a small number of threats that has the potential to hold our society seriously at risk and might result in defeat of our military forces.

Briefly, a single nuclear weapon exploded at high altitude above the United States will interact with the Earth's atmosphere, ionosphere, and magnetic field to produce an electromagnetic pulse (EMP) radiating down to the Earth and additionally create electrical currents in the Earth. EMP effects are both direct and indirect. The former are due to electromagnetic "shocking" of electronics and stressing of electrical systems, and the latter arise from the damage that "shocked"—upset, damaged, and destroyed—electronics controls then inflict on the systems in which they are embedded. The indirect effects can be even more severe than the direct effects.

The electromagnetic fields produced by weapons designed and deployed with the intent to produce EMP have a high likelihood of damaging electrical power systems, electronics, and information systems upon which American society depends. Their effects on dependent systems and infrastructures could be sufficient to qualify as catastrophic to the Nation.

Depending on the specific characteristics of the attacks, unprecedented cascading failures of our major infrastructures could result. In that event, a regional or national recovery would be long and difficult and would seriously degrade the safety and overall viability of our Nation. The primary avenues for catastrophic damage to the Nation are through our electric power infrastructure and thence into our telecommunications, energy, and other infrastructures. These, in turn, can seriously impact other important aspects of our Nation's life, including the financial system; means of getting food, water, and medical care to the citizenry; trade; and production of goods and services. The recovery of any one of the key national infrastructures is dependent on the recovery of others. The longer the outage, the more problematic and uncertain the recovery will be. It is possible for the functional outages to become mutually reinforcing until at some point the degradation of infrastructure could have irreversible effects on the country's ability to support its population.

EMP effects from nuclear bursts are not new threats to our nation. The Soviet Union in the past and Russia and other nations today are potentially capable of creating these effects. Historically, this application of nuclear weaponry was mixed with a much larger population of nuclear devices that were the primary source of destruction, and thus EMP as a weapons effect was not the primary focus. Throughout the Cold War, the United States did not try to protect its civilian infrastructure against either the physical or EMP impact of nuclear weapons, and instead depended on deterrence for its safety.

What is different now is that some potential sources of EMP threats are difficult to deter—they can be terrorist groups that have no state identity, have only one or a few weapons, and are motivated to attack the US without regard for their own safety. Rogue states, such as North Korea and Iran, may also be developing the capability to pose an EMP threat to the United States, and may also be unpredictable and difficult to deter.

Certain types of relatively low-yield nuclear weapons can be employed to generate potentially catastrophic EMP effects over wide geographic areas, and designs for variants of such weapons may have been illicitly trafficked for a quarter-century.

China and Russia have considered limited nuclear attack options that, unlike their Cold War plans, employ EMP as the primary or sole means of attack. Indeed, as recently as May 1999, during the NATO bombing of the former Yugoslavia, high-ranking members of the Russian Duma, meeting with a US congressional delegation to discuss the Balkans conflict, raised the specter of a Russian EMP attack that would paralyze the United States.

Another key difference from the past is that the US has developed more than most other nations as a modern society heavily dependent on electronics, telecommunications, energy, information networks, and a rich set of financial and transportation systems that leverage modern technology. This asymmetry is a source of substantial economic, industrial, and societal advantages, but it creates vulnerabilities and critical interdependencies that are potentially disastrous to the United States. Therefore, terrorists or state actors that possess relatively unsophisticated missiles armed with nuclear weapons may well calculate that, instead of destroying a city or military base, they may obtain the greatest political-military utility from one or a few such weapons by using them—or threatening their use—in an EMP attack. The current vulnerability of US critical infrastructures can both invite and reward attack if not corrected;

however, correction is feasible and well within the Nation's means and resources to accomplish.

WE CAN PREVENT AN EMP CATASTROPHE

The Nation's vulnerability to EMP that gives rise to potentially large-scale, long-term consequences can be reasonably and readily reduced below the level of a potentially catastrophic national problem by coordinated and focused effort between the private and public sectors of our country. The cost for such improved security in the next 3 to 5 years is modest by any standard—and extremely so in relation to both the war on terror and the value of the national infrastructures involved. The appropriate response to this threatening situation is a balance of prevention, protection, planning, and preparations for recovery. Such actions are both rational and feasible. A number of these actions also reduce vulnerabilities to other serious threats to our infrastructures, thus giving multiple benefits.

NATURE OF THE EMP THREAT

High-altitude EMP results from the detonation of a nuclear warhead at altitudes of about 40 to 400 kilometers above the Earth's surface. The immediate effects of EMP are disruption of, and damage to, electronic systems and electrical infrastructure. EMP is not reported in the scientific literature to have direct effects on people in the parameter range of present interest.

EMP and its effects were observed during the US and Soviet atmospheric test programs in 1962. Figure 1 depicts the Starfish nuclear detonation—not designed or intended as a generator of EMP—at an altitude of about 400 kilometers above Johnston Island in the Pacific Ocean. Some electronic and electrical systems in the Hawaiian Islands, 1400 kilometers distant, were affected, causing the failure of street-lighting systems, tripping of circuit breakers, triggering of burglar alarms, and damage to a telecommunications relay facility. In their testing that year, the Soviets executed a series of nuclear detonations in which they exploded 300 kiloton weapons at approximately 300, 150, and 60 kilometers above their test site in South Central Asia. They report that on each shot they observed damage to overhead and underground buried cables at distances of

600 kilometers. They also observed surge arrestor burnout, spark-gap breakdown, blown fuses, and power supply breakdowns.

What is significant about an EMP attack is that one or a few high-altitude nuclear detonations can produce EMP effects that can potentially disrupt or damage electronic and electrical systems over much of the United States, virtually simultaneously, at a time determined by an adversary.

Gamma rays from a high-altitude nuclear detonation interact with the atmosphere to produce a radio-frequency wave of unique, spatially varying intensity that covers everything within line-of-sight of the explosion's center point. It is useful to focus on three major EMP components.

FIRST EMP COMPONENT (E1)

The first component is a free-field energy pulse with a rise-time measured in the range of a fraction of a billionth to a few billionths of a second. It is the "electromagnetic shock" that disrupts or damages electronics-based control systems, sensors, communication systems, protective systems, computers, and similar devices. Its damage or functional disruption occurs essentially simultaneously over a very large area.

Widespread red air glow amid dark clouds, caused mostly by x-ray-excited atomic oxygen (i.e., oxygen by photoelectrons liberated by Starfish X-rays)

SECOND EMP COMPONENT (E2)

The middle-time component covers roughly the same geographic area as the first component and is similar to lightning in its time-dependence, but is far more geographically widespread in its character and somewhat lower in amplitude. In general, it would not be an issue for critical infrastructure systems since they have existing protective measures for defense against occasional lightning strikes. The most significant risk is synergistic, because the E2 component follows a small fraction of a second after the first component's insult, which has the ability to impair or destroy many protective and control features. The energy associated with the second component thus may be allowed to pass into and damage systems.

THIRD EMP COMPONENT (E3)

The final major component of EMP is a subsequent, slower-rising, longer-duration pulse that creates disruptive currents in long electricity transmission lines, resulting in damage to electrical supply and distribution systems connected to such lines (Figure 3). The sequence of E1, E2, and then E3 components of EMP is important because each can cause damage, and the later damage can be increased as a result of the earlier damage. About 70% of the total electrical power load of the United States is within the region exposed to the EMP event.

PREVENTION

An EMP attack is one way for a terrorist activity to use a small amount of nuclear weaponry—potentially just one weapon—in an effort to produce a catastrophic impact on our society, but it is not the only way. In addition, there are potential applications of surface-burst nuclear weaponry, biological and chemical warfare agents, and cyber attacks that might cause damage that could reach large-scale, long-term levels. The first order of business is to prevent any of these attacks from occurring.

The US must establish a global environment that will profoundly discourage such attacks. We must persuade nations to forgo obtaining nuclear weapons or to provide acceptable assurance that these weapons will neither threaten the vital interests of the United States nor fall into threatening hands.

For all others, we must make it difficult and dangerous to acquire the materials to make a nuclear weapon and the means to deliver them. We must hold at risk of capture or destruction anyone who has such weaponry, wherever they are in the world.

Those who engage in or support these activities must be made to understand that they do so at the risk of everything they value. Those who harbor or help those who conspire to create these weapons must suffer serious consequences as well.

In case these measures do not completely succeed, we must have vigorous interdiction and interception efforts to thwart delivery of all such weaponry. To support this strategy, the US must have intelligence capabilities sufficient to understand what is happening at each stage of developing threats. In summary, the costs of mounting such attacks must be made to be great in all respects, and the likelihood of successful attack rendered unattractively small.

The current national strategy for war on terrorism already contains all of these elements. The threat of an EMP attack further raises what may be at stake.

To further forestall an EMP attack, we must reduce our vulnerability to EMP and develop our ability to recover, should there be an attack, in order to reduce the incentives to use such weaponry. We should never allow terrorists or rogue states a "cheap shot" that has such a large and potentially devastating impact.

PROTECTION AND RECOVERY OF CIVILIAN INFRASTRUCTURES

Each critical infrastructure in the US is dependent upon other infrastructures. The interdependence on the proper functioning of such systems constitutes a hazard when threat of widespread failures exists. The strong interdependence of our critical national infrastructures may cause unprecedented challenges in attempts to recover from the widespread disruption and damage that would be caused by an EMP attack.

All of the critical functions of US society and related infrastructures—electric power, telecommunications, energy, financial, transportation, emergency services, water, food, etc.—have electronic devices embedded in most aspects of their systems, often providing critical controls. Electric power has thus emerged as an essential service underlying US society and all of its other critical infrastructures. Telecommunications has grown to a critical level but may not rise to the same level as electrical power in terms of risk to the Nation's survival. All other infrastructures and critical functions are dependent upon the support of electric power and telecommunications. Therefore, we must make special efforts to prepare and protect these two high-leverage systems.

Most critical infrastructure system vulnerabilities can be reduced below the level that potentially invites attempts to create a national catastrophe. By protecting key elements in each critical infrastructure and by preparing to recover essential services, the prospects for a terrorist or rogue state being able to achieve large-scale, long-term damage can be minimized. This can be accomplished reasonably and expeditiously.

Such preparation and protection can be achieved over the next few years, given a dedicated commitment by the federal government and an affordable investment of resources. We need to take actions and allocate resources to decrease the likelihood that catastrophic consequences from an EMP attack will occur, to reduce our current serious level of vulnerability to acceptable levels and thereby reduce incentives to attack, and to remain a viable modern society even if an EMP attack occurs. Since this is a matter of national security, the federal government must shoulder the responsibility of managing the most serious infrastructure vulnerabilities.

Homeland Security Presidential Directives 7 and 8 lay the authoritative basis for the Federal government to act vigorously and coherently to mitigate many of the risks to the Nation from terrorist attack. The effects of EMP on our major infrastructures lie within these directives, and the directives specify adequate responsibilities and provide sufficient authorities to deal with the civilian sector consequences of an EMP attack.

In particular, the Department of Homeland Security (DHS) has been established, led by a Secretary with authority, responsibility, and the obligation to request needed resources for the mission of protecting the US and recovering from the impacts of the most serious threats. This official must assure that plans, resources, and implementing structures are in place to accomplish these objectives, specifically with respect to the EMP threat. In doing so, DHS must work in conjunction with the other established governmental institutions and with experts in the private sector to most efficiently accomplish this mission. It is important that metrics for assessing improvements in prevention, protection, and recovery be put in place and then evaluated and that progress be reported regularly. DHS must clearly and expeditiously delineate its responsibility and actions in relation to other governmental institutions and the private sector, in order to provide clear accountability and avoid confusion and duplication of effort.

Specific recommendations are provided below with respect to both the particulars for securing each of the most critical national infrastructures against EMP threats and the governing principles for addressing these issues of national survival and recovery in the aftermath of EMP attack.

It will not be possible to reduce the incentives for an EMP attack to an acceptable level of risk through defensive protection measures alone. It is possible to achieve an acceptable level of risk and reduced invitation to an EMP attack with a strategy of:

- Pursuing intelligence, interdiction, and deterrence to discourage EMP attack against the US and its interests

- Protecting critical components of the infrastructure, with particular emphasis on those that, if damaged, would require long periods of time to repair or replace

- Maintaining the capability to monitor and evaluate the condition of critical infrastructures

- Recognizing an EMP attack and understanding how its effects differ from other forms of infrastructure disruption and damage

- Planning to carry out a systematic recovery of critical infrastructures

- Training, evaluating, "Red Teaming," and periodically reporting to the Congress

- Defining the Federal Government's responsibility and authority to act

- Recognizing the opportunities for shared benefits

- Conducting research to better understand infrastructure system effects and developing cost-effective solutions to manage these effects

The cost for such improved security in the next 3 to 5 years is modest by any standard—and extremely so in relation to both the war on terror and the value of the national infrastructures involved. Costs at later times may be adjusted to deal with the then-apparent threat and future levels of effort required.

INTELLIGENCE, INTERDICTION, AND DETERRENCE

The federal government's efforts to establish and maintain a global environment that profoundly discourages potentially catastrophic attacks is our first line of defense. The development, trading, and movement of critical materials and weapons useful for mounting WMD attacks, including those that are based on the use of EMP, must be identified as early in the process as possible. The methods and materials that could encourage an EMP attack must be added to the list of threats presently being sought out and annihilated. The US and its allies against transnational terrorism must make it exceedingly difficult and dangerous for organizations to position themselves to be a threat, or allow others to use their country and its assets in order to become a threat, specifically including EMP threats. We must hold potential perpetrators at risk of capture or destruction, whenever and wherever in the world they operate.

PROTECTING CRITICAL COMPONENTS OF THE INFRASTRUCTURE

Some components of critical infrastructures, such as large turbines, generators, and high-voltage transformers in electrical power systems, and electronic switching systems in telecommunication systems, would require long periods of time to repair or replace. These components should be configured so that even under electronic disruption and damage, such as could be produced by EMP, they do not become further damaged in the course of shutting down or attempting to restore themselves. This type of damage has occurred in the past. During the Northeast power blackout of 1965, Consolidated Edison generators, transformers, motors, and auxiliary equipment were damaged by the sudden shutdown. In particular, the #3 unit at the Ravenswood power plant in New York City suffered damage when the blackout caused loss of oil pressure to the main turbine bearing. The damage kept that unit out of service for nearly a year, and more immediately, complicated and delayed the restoration of service to New York City.

MAINTAINING THE CAPABILITY TO MONITOR AND EVALUATE THE CONDITION OF CRITICAL INFRASTRUCTURES

After an EMP attack, system operators and others in positions of authority and responsibility must have immediate access to information sufficient to characterize the state of their critical infrastructure systems. Without such system monitoring and reporting information, the system operators will not have the information required to evaluate the extent of the loss of infrastructure and know how to begin restoration of their systems. They may even induce further damage by taking inappropriate actions or failing to take necessary actions. During the time leading up to the August 14, 2003, Midwest power blackout that affected both the United States and Canada, key system operators did not have a functioning alarm system, did not recognize that the alarm system was not functioning, and had only fragmentary information on the changing configuration of the rapidly collapsing power grid for which they were responsible.

RECOGNIZING EMP ATTACK

Electronic upsets and failures occur under normal operating circumstances, even in high-reliability equipment such as that supporting critical infrastructure. EMP-induced upsets and failures, however, are different from those encountered in the normal operation of infrastructure systems, and in fact have unique aspects not encountered under any other circumstances.

EMP produces nearly simultaneous upset and damage of

electronic and of other electrical equipment over wide geographic areas, determined by the altitude, character, and explosive yield of the EMP-producing nuclear explosion. Since such upset and damage is not encountered in other circumstances and particularly not remotely to the same scale, the normal experience of otherwise skilled system operators and others in positions of responsibility and authority will not have prepared them to identify what has happened to the system, what actions to take to minimize further adverse consequences, and what actions must be carried out to restore the impacted systems as swiftly and effectively as possible.

Special system capabilities and operator awareness, planning, training, and testing will be required to deal with EMP-induced system impacts. The first requirement is for the operators of critical infrastructure systems to be able to determine that a high-altitude nuclear explosion has occurred and has produced a unique set of adverse effects on their systems. That information can be provided by local electromagnetic sensors, by information from Earth satellite systems, or by other means. Whatever the means, the operators and others in positions of authority and responsibility must receive the information immediately. Therefore, the EMP event notification system must itself be highly reliable during and after an EMP attack.

Operators and others in positions of authority and responsibility must be trained to recognize that an EMP attack in fact has taken place, to understand the wide range of effects it can produce, to analyze the status of their infrastructure systems, to avoid further system degradation, to dispatch resources to begin effective system restoration, and to sustain the most critical functions while the system is being repaired and restored. Failures similar to those induced by EMP do not occur in normal system operation; therefore, the training for, and experience developed in the course of, normal system operation will not provide operators with the skills and knowledge base necessary to perform effectively after EMP-induced system disruption and failure. Training, procedures, simulations, and exercises must be developed and carried out that are specifically designed to contend with EMP-induced effects.

PLANNING TO CARRY OUT A SYSTEMATIC RECOVERY OF CRITICAL INFRASTRUCTURES

A crisis such as the immediate aftermath of an EMP attack is not the time to begin planning for an effective response. Plans to avoid causing further damage to critical infrastructures and to carry out a systematic recovery of those infrastructures must be in hand at the earliest possible time. Planning for responding to an EMP attack should begin now and should be carried out jointly by system operators, hardware and software providers, and experts in both the government and private sectors.

Individual infrastructure systems have many similar electronically based control and monitoring functions. The primary features of EMP attack mitigation in each infrastructure include elements of protection of critical functions, identifying where damage within the system is located, dispatch/allocation of resources to allow for timely restoration and development of operational procedures including simulation of both individual and interacting infrastructures, training, testing, and governance. This requires test and evaluation of both existing and future systems to identify weak spots subject to EMP damage and focus mitigation activities accordingly. EMP protection thus has a substantial aspect focused on individual functioning units within each system that contains electronic components, although not necessarily on the individual electronic subcomponents of these units themselves. These units include distributed Supervisory Control and Data Acquisition (SCADA) modules, mobile communicators, radios, embedded control computers, etc. New units can be EMP-hardened for a very small fraction of the cost of the non-hardened item, e.g., 1% to 3% of cost, if hardening is done at the time the unit is designed and manufactured. In contrast, retrofitting existing functional components is potentially an order of magnitude more expensive and should be done only for critical system units. It is important to note, however, that for protection to remain functional, it must be tested and maintained in its operational mode with rigor and discipline.

TRAINING, EVALUATING, RED TEAMING, AND

PERIODICALLY REPORTING TO THE CONGRESS

Identifying an EMP attack, understanding the state of the system after attack, developing and implementing plans for system restoration, and having operators and others in positions of authority and responsibility trained to recognize and respond effectively are elements of strategy that are common to managing the effects of EMP for each of the Nation's critical infrastructure components. Conducting and evaluating the results of training, simulations, tests, and Red Team activities, and periodically reporting the results to senior executive branch leaders, the Congress, and the public are important elements of being well-prepared for EMP attack, which in turn will sharply reduce the incentives for conduct of such an attack.

DEFINING THE FEDERAL GOVERNMENT'S RESPONSIBILITY AND AUTHORITY TO ACT

Governance of the critical infrastructures such as electrical power systems and communications is presently distributed among statutory governmental entities at the federal, state, regional, and municipal levels, as well as among a variety of non-governmental entities. A multiplicity of statutory bodies, private companies, associations, and individual owners also participate in determining decisions and actions. Nevertheless, the process is coordinated, albeit loosely, to produce normal efficient, reliable, and high quality service that is the envy of the world—in a peacetime environment.

A terrorist threat—let alone a terrorist attack—is outside the ambit of normal governance of the key national infrastructures. In dealing with such threats, the Department of Homeland Security has the unique and sole responsibility and authority to govern the specific actions and involved parties within the US, including requesting enabling Congressional funding as appropriate and necessary. DHS must interact with other governmental institutions and the private sector in defining liability, responsibility and funding in order to enable private and government facilities, such as independent power plants, to contribute their capability in a time of national need, yet not interfere with market creation and operation to the maximum extent practical.

Industry associations, system owners/providers, private consultants, and universities all will be able to contribute useful levels of knowledge and skills. DHS is responsible for making the prudent trade-offs within each mitigation activity between performance, risk, schedule, and cost in relation to consequent system protection and then-expected risk in order to achieve maximum protection. For example, some actions taken to protect a system from an EMP attack may diminish the reliability or quality of that system's normal commercial performance, while other actions may improve the performance.

As an example of resources readily available to DHS with respect to the electric system, the North American Reliability Counsel (NERC) and the Electric Power Research Institute are well-positioned to provide much of the support needed in regard to the EMP threat. Working closely with industry and these institutions, the DHS should provide for the necessary capability to control the national bulk electricity supply system in order to protect critical services, minimize its self-destruction in the event of an EMP attack, and recover its normal capabilities as rapidly and effectively as possible thereafter.

RECOGNIZING THE OPPORTUNITIES FOR SHARED BENEFITS

Most of the following initiatives and actions the Commission recommends militate against more than an EMP attack. The protection and/or rapid restoration of critical infrastructures in the civilian sector from an EMP attack also will be effective against other types of infrastructure disruptions, such as attacks aimed at directly damaging or destroying key components of the electrical system, and natural or accidental large-scale disruptions are also significantly mitigated by these same initiatives. Some of these steps also enhance reliability and quality of critical infrastructures, which is a major direct benefit to the US economy and to our way of life.

CONDUCTING RESEARCH AND DEVELOPMENT

Very little research and development addressing EMP-related system response protection and recovery issues has been done for more than a decade. Conducting research to better understand infrastructure system effects and developing cost-effective solutions to manage these effects will be important to understanding the implications of the rapid evolution of electronics and electrical systems, and their growing role in controlling and operating modern critical infrastructure.

ELECTRIC POWER INFRASTRUCTURE
NATURE OF THE PROBLEM

Electric power is integral to the functioning of electronic components. For highly reliable systems such as commercial and military telecommunications, electric power usually comes from batteries (in the short term), local emergency power supplies (generally over time-intervals of less then 72 hours), and electricity delivered through the local electrical utility ("power" lines in the home, office and factory). Local emergency power supplies are limited by supplies of stored fuel. Increasingly, locally stored fuel in buildings and cities is being reduced for fire safety and environmental pollution reasons, so that the emergency generation availability without refueling is limited.

Geomagnetic storms, a natural phenomenon driven by the solar wind, may, by a different physical mechanism, produce ground-induced currents (GIC) that can affect the electrical system in a manner similar to the E3 component of EMP. Disruptions caused by geomagnetic storms, such as the collapse of Quebec Hydro grid during the geomagnetic storm of 1989, have occurred many times

Depending on the explosive yield of the nuclear weapon used, EMP-induced GIC may be several times larger than that produced by the average geomagnetic storm, and may even be comparable to those expected to arise in the largest geomagnetic storm ever observed. It may also occur over an area not normally affected by historic geomagnetic storms.

The North American economy and the functioning of the society as a whole are critically dependent on the availability of electricity, as needed, where and when needed. The electric power system in the US and interconnected areas of Canada and Mexico is outstanding in terms of its ability to meet load demands with high quality and reliable electricity at reasonable cost. However, over the last decade or two, there has been relatively little large-capacity electric transmission constructed and the generation additions that have been made, while barely adequate, have been increasingly located considerable distances from load for environmental, political, and economic reasons. As a result, the existing National electrical system not infrequently operates at or very near local limits on its physical capacity to move power from generation to load. Therefore, the slightest insult or upset to the system can cause functional collapse affecting significant numbers of people, businesses, and manufacturing. It is not surprising that a single EMP attack may well encompass and degrade at least 70% of the Nation's electrical service, all in one instant.

The impact of such EMP is different and far more catastrophic than that effected by historic blackouts, in three primary respects:

1. The EMP impact is virtually instantaneous and occurs simultaneously over a much larger geographic area. Generally, there are neither precursors nor warning, and no opportunity for human-initiated protective action. The early-time EMP component is the "electromagnetic shock" that disrupts or damages electronics-based control systems and sensors, communication systems, protective systems, and control computers, all of which are used to control and bring electricity from generation sites to customer loads in the quantity and quality needed. The E1 pulse also causes some insulator flashovers in the lower-voltage electricity distribution systems (those found in suburban neighborhoods, in rural areas and inside cities), resulting in immediate broad-scale loss-of-load. Functional collapse of the power system is almost definite over the entire affected region, and may cascade into adjacent geographic areas.

2. The middle-time EMP component is similar to lightning in its time-dependence but is far more widespread in its character although of lower amplitude—essentially a great many lightning-type insults over a large geographic area which might obviate protection. The late-time EMP component couples very efficiently to long electrical

transmission lines and forces large direct electrical currents to flow in them, although they are designed to carry only alternating currents. The energy levels thereby concentrated at the ends of these long lines can become large enough to damage major electrical power system components. The most significant risk is synergistic, because the middle and late-time pulses follow after the early-time pulse, which can impair or destroy protective and control features of the power grid. Then the energies associated with the middle and late-time EMP thus may pass into major system components and damage them. It may also pass electrical surges or fault currents into the loads connected to the system, creating damage in national assets that are not normally considered part of the infrastructure per se. Net result is recovery times of months to years, instead of days to weeks.

3. Proper functioning of the electrical power system requires communication systems, financial systems, transportation systems, and—for much of the generation—continuous or nearly continuous supply of various fuels. However, the fuel-supply, communications, transportation, and financial infrastructures would be simultaneously disabled or degraded in an EMP attack and are dependent upon electricity for proper functioning. For electrical system recovery and restoration of service, the availability of these other infrastructures is essential. The longer the outage, the more problematic, and uncertainty-fraught the recovery will be.

The recent cascading outage of August 14, 2003, is an example of a single failure compounded by system weaknesses and human mistakes. It also provides an example of the effectiveness of protective equipment. However, with EMP there are multiple insults coupled with the disabling of protective devices simultaneously over an extremely broad region—damage to the system is likely and recovery slow.

RECOMMENDED MITIGATION AND RESPONSIBILITY

The electrical system is designed to break into "islands" of roughly matching generation and load when a portion of the system receives a severe electrical insult. This serves both to protect electricity supply in the non-impacted regions and to allow for the stable island-systems to be used to "restart" the island(s) that have lost functionality. With EMP, the magnitude, speed, and multi-faceted nature of the insult, its broad geographic reach, along with the number of simultaneous insults, and the adverse synergies all are likely to result in a situation where the islanding scheme will fail to perform as effectively as intended, if at all. Since the impacted geographic area is large, restoring the system from the still-functioning perimeter regions would take a great deal of time, possibly weeks to months at best. Indeed, the only practical way to restart much of the impacted electrical system may be with generation that can be started without an external power source. This is called "black start" generation and primarily includes hydroelectric (including pumped storage), geothermal, and independent diesel generators of modest capacity.

The recommended actions will substantially improve service and recovery during "normal" large-scale blackouts, and will critically enable recovery under EMP circumstances.

PROTECTION

It is impractical to protect the entire electrical power system from damage by an EMP attack. There are too many components of too many different types, manufacturers, designs, and vulnerabilities within too many jurisdictional entities, and the cost to retrofit is too great. Widespread functional collapse of the electrical power system in the area affected by EMP is possible in the face of a geographically broad EMP attack, with even a relatively few unprotected components in place. However, it is practical to reduce to low levels the probability of widespread damage to major power system components that require long times to replace. This will enable significantly improved recovery times, since it avoids the loss of long lead-time and critical components. It is important to protect the ability of the system to fragment gracefully into islands, to the extent practical in the particular EMP circumstance. This approach is cost-efficient and can leverage efforts to improve reliability of bulk electricity supply and enhance its security against the broader range of threats.

RESTORATION

The key to minimizing adverse effects from loss of electrical power is the speed of restoration. Restoration involves matching generation capacity to a load of equivalent size over a transmission network that is initially isolated from the broader system. The larger system is then functionally rebuilt by bringing that mini system, or "island," to the standard operating frequency and thereupon by adding more blocks of generation and load to this core in amounts that can be absorbed by the growing subsystem. This is a demanding and time-consuming process in the best of circumstances. In the singular circumstance of an EMP attack with multiple damaged components, related infrastructure failures, and particularly severe challenges in communications and transportation, the time required to restore electrical power is expected to be considerably longer than we have experienced in recent history.

However, by protecting key system components needed for restoration, by structuring the network to fail gracefully, and by creating a comprehensive prioritized recovery plan for the most critical power needs, the risk of an EMP attack having a catastrophic effect on the Nation can be greatly reduced. DHS must ensure that the mitigation plan is jointly developed by the federal government and the electric power industry, implemented fully, instilled into systems operations, and tested and practiced regularly to maintain a capability to respond effectively in emergencies. The North American Reliability Council and the Electric Power Research Institute are aptly positioned to provide much of what's needed to support DHS in carrying out its responsibilities. The US Energy Association is well-suited to coordinating activities between and among the various energy sectors that together affect the electric power system and its vitality.

ESSENTIAL COMPONENT PROTECTION

1. Assure protection of high-value long-lead-time transmission assets.

2. Assure protection of high-value generation assets. System-level protection assurance is more complex due to the need for multiple systems to function in proper sequence.

3. Assure Key Generation Capability. Not all plants can or should be protected. However, regional evaluation of key generating resources necessary for recovery should be selected and protected.

a. Coal-fired generation plants make up nearly half the Nation's generation and are generally the most robust overall to EMP, with many electromechanical controls still in operation. Such coal plants also normally have at least a few days to a month of on-site fuel storage.

b. Natural gas-fired combustion turbines and associated steam secondary systems represent the newest and a significant contributor to meeting loads. These have modern electronics-based control and thus are more vulnerable. Natural gas is not stored on-site and likely will be interrupted in an EMP attack. However, provision can be made to have gas-fired plants also operate on fuel oil; many do already.

c. Nuclear plants produce roughly 20% of the Nation's generation and have many redundant fail-safe systems that tend to remove them from service whenever any system upset is sensed. Their safe shut down should be assured, but they will be unavailable until near the end of restoration.

d. Hydroelectric power is generally quite robust to EMP, and constitutes a substantial fraction of total national generation capacity, albeit unevenly distributed geographically.

e. In general, the various distributed and renewable fueled generators are not significant enough at this time to warrant special protection.

f. Black start generation of all types is critical and will need to be protected from EMP upset or damage.

4. Assure functional integrity of critical communications channels. The most critical communications channels in the power grid are the ones that enable recovery from collapse, such as ones that enable manual operation and coordination-supporting contacts between

distant system operators and those that support system diagnostics. Generation, switching, and load dispatch communications support is next in importance.

5. Assure availability of emergency power at critical facilities needed for restoration. Transmission substations need uninterruptible power to support rapid restoration of grid connectivity and operability, and thereby to more quickly restore service. Most have short-life battery backup systems, but relatively few have longer-duration emergency generators; much more emphasis on the latter is needed.

6. Assure protection of fuel production and its delivery for generation. Fuel supply adequate to maintain critical electrical service and to restore expanded service is critical.

7. Expand and assure intelligent islanding capability. The ability of the larger electrical power system to break into relatively small subsystem islands is important to mitigate overall EMP impacts and provide faster restoration.

8. Develop and deploy system test standards and equipment. Device-level robustness standards and test equipment exist, but protection at the system level is the overarching goal. System-level robustness improvements such as isolators, line protection, and grounding improvements will be the most practical and least expensive in most cases relative to replacement with more robust individual component devices. Periodic testing of system response is necessary.

SYSTEM RESTORATION

1. Develop and enable a restoration plan. This plan must prioritize the rapid restoration of power to government-identified critical service. Sufficient black start generation capacity must be provided where it is needed in the associated subsystem islands, along with transmission system paths that can be isolated and connected to matching loads. The plan must address outages with wide geographic coverage, multiple major component failures, poor communication capabilities, and widespread failure of islanding schemes within the EMP-affected area. Government and industry responsibilities must

be unequivocally and completely assigned. All necessary legal and financial arrangements, e.g., for indemnification, must be put into place to allow industry to implement specified government priorities with respect to service restoration, as well as to deal with potential environmental and technical hazards in order to assure rapid recovery.

2. Simulate, train, exercise, and test the plan. Simulators must be developed for use in training and developing procedures similar to those in the airline industry; a handful should suffice for the entire country. Along with simulation and field exercises, Red Team discipline should be employed to surface weaknesses and prioritize their rectification.

3. Assure sufficient numbers of adequately trained recovery personnel.

4. Assure availability of replacement equipment. R&D is under way—and should be vigorously pursued—into the production of emergency "universal" replacements. The emergency nature of such devices would trade efficiency and service-life for modularity, transportability, and affordability.

5. Implement redundant backup diagnostics and communication. Assure that system operators can reliably identify and locate damaged components.

TELECOMMUNICATIONS
IMPORTANCE OF ASSURED TELECOMMUNICATIONS

Telecommunications plays a key role in US society in terms of its direct effect on individuals and business and due to its impact on other key infrastructures. The relationship of telecommunications to the other critical infrastructures, such as the financial industry, is often recognized during and following widespread outages, such as those experienced as a result of the September 11, 2001, attacks on the World Trade Centers and the immediate vicinity of "Ground Zero." The local disruption of all critical infrastructures, including power, transportation, and telecommunications, interrupted operations in key financial markets and posed increased liquidity risks to the US financial system. In the days following the attacks, institutions in the affected areas were implementing their business continuity plans, which proved vital to the rapid restoration and recovery of services in the New York City area. In addition, the President emphasized that the prompt restoration of Wall Street's capabilities was critical to the economic welfare of the Nation; in doing so, he aptly linked economic stability to national security.

For some of the most critical infrastructure services, such as electric power, natural gas, and financial services, assured communications are essential to their recovery following a major adverse event. The importance of telecommunications in an emergency situation is underscored by the existence of the National Communications System (NCS), established by Executive Order 12472, *Assignment of National Security and Emergency Preparedness Telecommunications Functions.*

The NCS shall seek to ensure that a national telecommunications infrastructure is developed which: (1) Is responsive to the national security and emergency preparedness needs of the President and the Federal departments, agencies and other entities, including telecommunications in support of national security leadership and continuity of government; (2) Is capable of satisfying priority telecommunications requirements under all circumstances through use of commercial, government and privately owned telecommunications resources; (3) Incorporates the necessary combination of hardness, redundancy, mobility, connectivity, interoperability, restorability and security to obtain, to the maximum extent Coordinating Center (NCC) for Telecommunications to facilitate the initiation, coordination, restoration, and reconstitution of National Security and Emergency Preparedness (NS/EP) telecommunications services or facilities under all crises and emergencies; developing and ensuring the implementation of plans and programs that support the viability of telecommunications infrastructure hardness, redundancy, mobility, connectivity, and security; and serving as the focal point for joint industry-government and interagency NS/EP telecommunications planning and partnerships. In addition, the President's National Security Telecommunications Advisory Committee (NSTAC), a Federal Advisory Committee Act (FACA) CEO-level advisory group to the President, is tasked with providing industry-sourced advice and expertise related to implementing policies affecting NS/EP communications. These NS/EP services are those "critical to the maintenance of a state of readiness or the response to and management of any event or crisis that causes harm or could cause harm to the population, damage to or the loss of property, or degrades or threatens the NS/EP posture of the United States."

The NSTAC in its 1985 Report on EMP found that "consistent with its cost constraints, industry should incorporate low-cost EMP mitigation practices into new facilities and, as appropriate, into upgrade programs. For those areas where a carrier/supplier recognizes that a significant improvement in EMP resistance and surveillance could be achieved, but at a cost beyond the carrier/supplier's own cost constraints, the carrier/supplier should identify such options to the government for evaluation and possible funding." On October 9, 1985, the NSTAC approved the EMP Final Task Force Report and forwarded a recommendation to the President, calling for a joint industry and Government program to reduce the costs of existing techniques for mitigating high-altitude electromagnetic pulse (HEMP)-induced transients and to develop new techniques for limiting transient effects. As a result, the NCS and industry, working with the ATIS—the Alliance for Industry Solutions—developed a set of ANSI standards and Generic Requirements[4] to address EMP.

NS/EP Definitions

NS/EP Telecommunications Services: Telecommunications services that are used to maintain a state of readiness or to respond to and manage any event or crisis (local, national, or international) that causes or could cause injury or harm to the population, damage to or loss of property, or degrades or loss of property, or degrades or threatens the NS/EP posture of the United States. (*"Telecommunications Service Priority [TSP] System for National Security*

Emergency Preparedness: Service User Manual," NCS Manual 3-1-1, July 9, 1990. Appendix A.)

NS/EP Requirements: Features that maintain a state of readiness or respond to and manage an event or crisis (local, national, or international), which causes or could cause injury or harm to the population, damage to or loss of property, or degrade or threaten the NS/EP posture of the United States. *(Federal Standard 1037C)*

With respect to NS/EP telecommunications, capabilities exist for prioritizing phone calls through the wireline, wireless, and satellite networks during the time interval when call volumes are excessive and facilities are damaged, giving priority to restoring services that may be damaged or degraded, and getting new circuits into operation.

According to recent testimony by a DHS official, "The NCS is continuing a diverse set of mature and evolving programs designed to ensure priority use of telecommunications services by NS/EP users during times of national crisis. The more mature services—including the Government Emergency Telecommunications Service (GETS) and the Telecommunications Service Priority (TSP)—were instrumental in the response to the September 11 attacks. FY 2005 funding enhances these programs and supports the development of the Wireless Priority Service (WPS) program and upgrade to the Special Routing Arrangement Service (SRAS). Specifically, priority service programs include: (1) GETS, which offers nationwide priority voice and low-speed data service during an emergency or crisis situation; (2) WPS, which provides a nationwide priority cellular service to key NS/EP users, including individuals from federal, state and local governments and the private sector; (3) TSP, which provides the administrative and operational framework for priority provisioning and restoration of critical NS/EP telecommunications services; (4) SRAS, which is a variant of GETS to support the Continuity of Government (COG) program including the reengineering of SRAS in the AT&T network and development of SRAS capabilities in the MCI and Sprint networks, and; (5) the Alerting and Coordination Network (ACN), which is an NCS program that provides dedicated communications between selected critical government and telecommunications industry operations centers."[6]

For example, due to concerns with respect to getting calls through during intervals of high network call volumes that follow disaster events, the Nuclear Regulatory Commission (NRC) utilizes the Government Emergency Telecommunications System (GETS) and other NS/EP telecom services such as wireless priority services to communicate with commercial nuclear power plants and to relay critical status information. This use of GETS grew out of lessons learned from the Three Mile Island incident in 1979. During the initial days of this incident, NRC personnel experienced communication problems that were attributed primarily to call volume overload at the local telephone company switch.

Another NS/EP service is the Telecommunications Service Priority (TSP) program, which exists to assign priority provisioning and restoration of critical NS/EP telecommunications services in the hours immediately following a major disaster. In place since the mid-1980s, more than 50,000 circuits are protected today under TSP, including circuits associated with critical infrastructures such as electric power, telecommunications, and financial services.

The telecommunication system consists of four basic and primary physical systems: wireline, wireless, satellite, and radio. In general, the national telecommunications infrastructure may be farther advanced then others in its ability to address the particular consequences of EMP. This is due in large measure to the recognized alternative threats to this system, as well as broad recognition of its importance to society. The three primary and separate systems (excluding radio) that make up the broad telecommunications infrastructure each provide specialized services; they also overlap heavily. Thus the loss or degradation of any one of these somewhat redundant subsystems subjects the remaining functional subsystems to heavier service loads.

Each of these four primary systems is unique in their capability to suffer insult from EMP. The wireline system is robust but will be degraded within the area exposed to the EMP electromagnetic fields. The wireless system is technologically fragile in relation to EMP, certainly in comparison to the wireline one. In general, it may be so seriously degraded in the EMP region as to be unavailable. Low Earth Orbit (LEO) communications satellites may also suffer radiation damage as a result of one or more high-altitude nuclear bursts that produce EMP (see Space Systems, page 44).

The radio communication sub-system of the national telecommunications infrastructure is not widespread, but where it is connected to antennas, power lines, telephone lines, or other extended conductors, it is also subject to substantial EMP damage. However, radio communication devices not so connected or not connected to such conductors at the time of the EMP attack are likely to be operable in the post-attack interval.

EMP EFFECTS ON TELECOMMUNICATIONS

Based upon results of Commission-sponsored testing, an EMP attack would disrupt or damage a functionally significant fraction of the electronic circuits in the Nation's civilian telecommunications systems in the region exposed to EMP. The remaining operational networks would be subjected to high levels of call attempts for some period of time after the attack, leading to degraded telecommunications services.

Key government and civilian personnel will need priority access to use public network resources to coordinate and support local, regional, and national recovery efforts, especially during the interval of severe network congestion.

To offset the temporary loss of electric power, telecommunications sites now utilize a mix of batteries, mobile generators, and fixed-location generators. These typically have between 4 and 72 hours of backup power available, and thus will depend on either the resumption of electrical utility power or fuel deliveries to function for longer periods of time.

For some of the most critical infrastructure services such as electric power, natural gas, and financial services, assured communications are necessary—but aren't necessarily sufficient—to the survival of that service during the initial time-intervals after an EMP attack. Therefore, a systematic approach to protecting or restoring key communications systems will be required.

RECOMMENDED MITIGATION ACTIVITIES

The following actions are recommended as particularly effective ones for mitigating the impacts of EMP attack:

- Expand the respective roles of the National Communications System (NCS) and the Defense Threat Reduction Agency (DTRA) as the Federal Focal Point for EMP within the Code of Federal Regulations Part 215 to address infrastructure interdependencies related to NS/EP telecommunications services.

- Ensure services targeted at NS/EP operate effectively as new technology is introduced into the telecommunications network. Specifically, services such as Government Emergency Telecommunications Service (GETS) and Wireless Priority Service (WPS) that are intended for use in emergency situations to improve the call completion probabilities for key personnel must operate effectively. Within the next 15 years, new technologies will be introduced into the public networks that will play major roles in operation of these services. EMP is just one of the potential threats that could stress the telecommunications networks; therefore, ensuring that NS/EP services perform effectively as new technology is introduced has benefits beyond providing robustness to EMP, and moreover is consistent with avoiding failures from other hostile actions.

- Determine the effects of EMP on different types of telecommunication equipment and facilities, using tests and theoretical analyses of the type done in the course of

Commission-sponsored work and previous EMP-related studies conducted by the National Communications System (NCS). A comprehensive, continuing telecommunications testing program, along with the use of existing national and international standards, may be a model activity that would be a key part of this overall National effort.

- Improve the ability of key network assets to survive HEMP. There are key elements in the network such as the Signal Transfer Points (STPs) in the signaling system (Signaling System 7 (SS7)), Home Location Register (HLR), and Visiting Location Register (VLR) in the wireless networks whose degradation can result in the loss of service to a larger number of users. Effective mitigation strategies include a combination of site hardening and installation of protective measures for the fast rise-time (E1) component of EMP.

- Improve the ability of telecommunications to withstand the sustained loss of utility-supplied electric power. This mitigation strategy would entail the use of best practices, review and improvement of existing programs such as the Telecommunications Electric Service Priority (TESP) program, and the increased use of alternative backup power sources.

- Conduct exercises to refine contingency operations. Conduct exercises that test and provide for improved contingency operations, assuming widespread multi-infrastructure degradation. The adequacy of mutual aid agreements, cross-organizational planning and coordination, and critical asset prioritization are examples of elements that should be tested and developed.

Managers of these critical services must design their systems and operating procedures to take into account the potential vulnerabilities introduced by EMP-driven failure of telecommunications devices and sub-systems.

BANKING AND FINANCE
NATURE OF THE PROBLEM

The financial services industry comprises a network of organizations and attendant systems that process instruments of monetary value in the form of deposits, loans, funds transfers, savings, and other financial transactions. It includes banks and other depository institutions, including the Federal Reserve System; investment-related companies such as underwriters, brokerages, and mutual funds; industry utilities such as the New York Stock Exchange, the Automated Clearing House, and the Society for Worldwide Interbank Financial Telecommunications; and third party processors that provide electronic processing services to financial institutions, including data and network management and check processing.

Virtually all American economic activity depends upon the functioning of the financial services industry. Today, most financial transactions that express National wealth are performed and recorded electronically. Virtually all transactions involving banks and other financial institutions happen electronically. Essentially all record-keeping of financial transactions involves information stored electronically. The financial services industry has evolved to the point that it would be impossible to operate without the efficiencies, speeds, and processing and storage capabilities of electronic information technology.

The terrorist attacks of September 11, 2001, demonstrated the vulnerabilities arising from the significant interdependencies of the Nation's critical infrastructures. The attacks disrupted all critical infrastructures in New York City, including power, transportation, and telecommunications. Consequently, operations in key financial markets were interrupted, increasing liquidity risks for the United States financial system.

The Interagency Paper, which was jointly issued by the Office of the Comptroller of the Currency (OCC), the Federal Reserve Board (FRB), and the Securities and Exchange Commission (SEC), specifies clearing and settlement systems as the most critical business operations at risk for financial markets. Because financial markets are highly interdependent, a wide-scale disruption of core clearing and settlement processes would have an immediate systemic effect on critical financial markets.

Moreover, in December 2002, the FRB revised its policy and procedures for NS/EP telecommunications programs administered by the National Communications System (NCS) to identify those functions supporting the Federal Reserve's NS/EP mission to maintain national liquidity. The FRB expanded the scope of services that would seriously affect continued financial operations if a telecommunications disruption of "a few minutes to one day" occurred. These functions, which are listed below, require same-day recovery and are critical to the operation and liquidity of banks and the stability of financial markets:

- Large-value inter-bank funds transfer, securities transfer, or payment-related services, such as FedWire, Clearing House Interbank Payments System (CHIPS), and the Society for Worldwide Interbank Financial Telecommunications (SWIFT)

- Automated clearinghouse (ACH) operators

- Key clearing and settlement utilities

- Treasury automated auction and processing system

- Large-dollar participants of these systems and utilities

The increasing dependence of the United States on an electronic economy, so beneficial to the creation and preservation of wealth, also adds to the adverse effects that would be produced by an EMP attack. The electronic technologies that are the foundation of the financial infrastructure are potentially vulnerable to EMP. These systems are also potentially vulnerable to EMP indirectly through other critical infrastructures, such as the electric power grid and telecommunications.

RECOMMENDED MITIGATION AND RESPONSIBILITY

Securing the financial services industry from the EMP threat is vital to the national security of the United States. The Federal government must assure that this system can survive sufficiently to preclude serious, long-term consequences.

The Department of Homeland Security, the Federal Reserve Board, and the Department of the Treasury, in cooperation with other relevant agencies, must develop contingency plans to ride out and recover key financial systems promptly from an EMP attack.

Key financial services include those means and resources that provide the general population with cash, credit, and other liquidity required to buy food, fuel, and other essential goods and services. We must protect the Nation's financial networks, banking records, and data retrieval systems that support cash, check, credit, debit, and other transactions through judicious balance of hardening, redundancy, and contingency plans.

The Federal government must work with the private sector to assure the protection and effective recovery of essential financial records and services infrastructure components from all deliberate adverse events, including EMP attack. Implementation of the recommendations made by the Department of the Treasury, the FRB, and the SEC in their *Interagency Paper on Sound Practices to Strengthen the Resilience of the US Financial System* to meet sabotage and cyber-threats that could engender requirements for protection and recovery should be expanded to include expeditious recovery from EMP attack:

- "Every organization in the financial services industry should identify all clearing and settlement activities in each critical financial market in which it is a core clearing and settlement organization or plays a significant role" that could be threatened by EMP attack.

- Industry should "determine appropriate recovery and resumption objectives for clearing and settlement activities in support of critical markets" following an EMP attack.

- Industry should be prepared to cope with an EMP attack by maintaining "sufficient geographically dispersed resources to meet recovery and resumption objectives.... Backup sites should not rely on the same infrastructure components (e.g., transportation, telecommunications, water supply, electric power) used by the primary site. Moreover, the operation of such sites should not be impaired by a wide-scale evacuation at or inaccessibility of staff that service the primary site."

- Industry should, "Routinely use or test recovery and resumption arrangements.... It is critical for firms to test backup facilities of markets, core clearing and settlement organizations, and third-party service providers to ensure connectivity, capacity, and the integrity of data transmission" against an EMP attack.

FUEL/ENERGY INFRASTRUCTURE

The vulnerabilities of this sector are produced by the responses of the electronic control systems that provide and utilize the near-real-time data flows needed to operate the fuel/energy infrastructure efficiently, as well as to identify and quickly react to equipment malfunctions or untoward incidents. EMP could also cause control or data-sensor malfunctions that are not easily discernible, leading to counterproductive operational decisions. Process control systems are critical to the operation and control of petroleum refineries, and little or no notice of an outage significantly increases the potential for damage during an emergency shutdown. Communications systems that are critical for operational control represent another locus of vulnerability. Communications are also critical in refineries to ensure safety of on-site personnel, the adjacent population, and the surrounding environment. The energy distribution infrastructure is also critically dependent on the availability of commercial power to operate the numerous pumps, valves and other electrical equipment that are required for a functional infrastructure.

DHS must develop a contingency plan that will provide strategy for protection and recovery for this sector, to include actions to be taken by both Government and industry. Government should establish a national inventory of parts for those items with long lead-times or that would be in demand in the event of a catastrophic event such as an EMP attack. The Energy Information Sharing and Analysis Center (ISAAC) should, with government funding, expand its mission to address EMP issues, and the government should work with the private sector to implement the general approach described in Strategy and Recommendations.

TRANSPORTATION INFRASTRUCTURE
NATURE OF THE PROBLEM

America's transportation sector is often addressed as a single infrastructure, but in reality its multiple modes provide for several separate infrastructures. Rail includes the freight railroad and commuter rail infrastructures; road includes the trucking and automobile infrastructures; water includes the maritime shipping and inland waterway infrastructures; and air includes the commercial and general aviation infrastructures.

As recognized by the President's National Security Telecommunications Advisory Committee (NSTAC) Information Infrastructure Group Report:

- The transportation industry is increasingly reliant on information technology and public information-transporting networks.

- Although a nationwide disruption of the transportation infrastructure may be unlikely, even a local or regional disruption could have a significant impact. Due to the diversity and redundancy of the US transportation system, the infrastructure is not at risk of nationwide disruption resulting from information system failure. Nonetheless, a disruption of the transportation information infrastructure on a regional or local scale has potential for widespread economic and national security effects.

- Marketplace pressures and increasing utilization of IT make large-scale, multimodal disruptions more likely in the future. As the infrastructure becomes more interconnected and interdependent, the transportation industry will increasingly rely on information technology to perform its most basic business functions. As this occurs, it becomes more likely that information system failures could result in large-scale disruptions of multiple modes of the transportation infrastructure.

- There is a need for a broad-based infrastructure assurance awareness program to assist all modes of transportation.

- The transportation industry could leverage ongoing research and development initiatives to improve the security of the transportation information infrastructure.

- There is a need for closer coordination between the transportation industry and other critical infrastructures.

The imperative to achieve superior performance has also led to a tremendous increase in the use of electronics that are potentially vulnerable to EMP. The internal combustion engine provides a familiar example of this phenomenon. Modern engines utilize electronics to increase performance, increase fuel efficiency, reduce emissions, increase diagnostic capability, and increase safety.

To gauge the degree of vulnerability of transportation infrastructures to EMP, the Commission has conducted an assessment of selected components of these infrastructures that are necessary to their operations. The assessment relied on testing where feasible, surveys and analyses for equipment and facilities for which testing was impractical, and reference to similarities to equipment for which EMP vulnerability data exists.

Based on this assessment, significant degradation of the transportation infrastructures are likely to occur in the immediate aftermath of an EMP attack. For example, municipal road traffic will likely be severely congested, possibly to the point of wide-area gridlock, as a result of traffic light malfunctions and the fraction of operating cars and trucks that will experience both temporary and in some cases unrecoverable engine shutdown. Railroad traffic will stop if communications with railroad control centers are lost or railway signals malfunction. Commercial air traffic will likely cease operations for safety and other traffic control reasons. Ports will stop loading and unloading ships until commercial power and cargo hauling infrastructures are restored.

The ability of the major transportation infrastructure components to recover depends on the plans in place and the availability of resources—including spare parts and support from other critical infrastructures upon which transportation is dependent. Transportation infrastructures have emergency response procedures in place; however, they do not explicitly address conditions that may exist for an EMP attack, such as little or no warning time and

245

simultaneous disruptions over wide areas. Restoration times will depend on the planning and training carried out, and on the availability of services from other infrastructures—notably power, fuel, and telecommunications.

STRATEGY FOR PROTECTION AND RECOVERY
RAILROADS

Railroad operations are designed to continue under stressed conditions. Backup power and provisioning is provided for operations to continue for days or even weeks at reduced capacity. However, some existing emergency procedures, such as transferring operations to backup sites, rely on significant warning time, such as may be received in a weather forecast before a hurricane. An EMP attack may occur without warning, thereby compromising the viability of available emergency procedures. Therefore, under the overall leadership of the DHS, the government and private sectors should work together to implement the general approach described in Strategy and Recommendations.

Specific actions should include:

- Heighten railroad officials' awareness of the possibility of EMP attack without warning that would produce wide-area, long-term disruption and damage to electronic systems.

- Perform test-based EMP assessments of railroad traffic control centers and retrofit modest EMP protection into these facilities, thereby minimizing the potential for adverse long term EMP effects. The emphasis of this effort should be on electronic control and telecommunication systems.

TRUCKING AND AUTOMOBILES

Emphasizing prevention and emergency clearing of traffic congestion in this area, DHS should coordinate a government and private sector program to:

- Initiate an outreach program to educate State and local authorities and traffic engineers on EMP effects and the expectation of traffic signal malfunctions, vehicle disruption and damage, and consequent traffic congestion.

- Work with municipalities to formulate recovery plans, including emergency clearing of traffic congestion and provisioning spare controller cards that could be used to repair controller boxes.

- Sponsor development of economical protection modules— preliminary results for which are already available from Commission-sponsored research—that could be retrofitted into existing traffic signal controller boxes and installed in new controller boxes during manufacture.

- Sponsor development of automobile robustness specifications and testing for EMP. These specifications should be implemented by augmenting existing specifications for gaining immunity to transient electromagnetic interference (EMI), rather than by developing separate specifications for EMP.

MARITIME SHIPPING

The essential port operations to be safeguarded are ship traffic control, cargo loading and unloading, and cargo storage and movement (incoming and outgoing). Ship traffic control is provided by the Coast Guard, which has robust backup procedures in place. Cargo storage and movement are covered by other transportation infrastructure recommendations. Therefore, focusing on cargo operations in this area, DHS should coordinate a government and private sector program to:

- Heighten port officials' awareness of the wide geographic coverage of EMP fields, the risk due to loss of commercial power for protracted time-intervals, and the need to evaluate the practicality of providing emergency generators for at least some portion of port and cargo operations.

- Assess the vulnerability of electric-powered loading/unloading equipment. Review the electromagnetic protection already in place for lightning, and require augmentation of this protection to provide significant EMP robustness.

- Coordinate findings with the "real-time" repair crews to ensure they are aware of the potential for EMP damage. Based on the assessment results, recommend spares provisions so that repairs can be made in a timely manner.

- Assess port data centers for the potential loss of data in electronic media. Provide useful measures of protection against EMP causing loss of function and/or data.

- Provide protected off-line spare parts and computers sufficient for minimum essential operations.

- Provide survivable radio and satellite communication capabilities for the Coast Guard and the Nation's ports.

COMMERCIAL AVIATION

In priority order, it must be ensured that airplanes caught in the air during an EMP attack can land safely, that critical recovery assets are protected, and that contingency plans for an extended no-fly period are developed. Thus, DHS should coordinate a government program in cooperation with the FAA to perform an operational assessment of the air traffic control system to identify a "thin-line" that provides the minimal essential capabilities necessary to return the air traffic control capability to at least a basic level of service after an EMP attack. Based on the results of this operational assessment, develop tactics for protection, operational workarounds, spares provisioning, and repairs to return to a minimum-essential service level.

FOOD INFRASTRUCTURE
NATURE OF THE PROBLEM

EMP can damage or disrupt the infrastructure that supplies food to the population of the United States. Recent federal efforts to better protect the food infrastructure from terrorist attack tend to focus on preventing small-scale disruption of the food infrastructure, such as would result from terrorists poisoning some food. Yet an EMP attack could potentially disrupt the food infrastructure over a large region encompassing many cities for a protracted period of weeks to months.

Technology has made possible a dramatic revolution in US agricultural productivity. The transformation of the United States from a nation of farmers to a nation where less than 2 percent of the population is able to feed the other 98 percent and supply export markets is made possible only by technological advancements that, since 1900, have increased the productivity of the modern farmer by more than 50-fold. Technology, in the form of knowledge, machines, modern fertilizers and pesticides, high-yield crops and feeds, is the key to this revolution in food production. Much of the technology for food production directly or indirectly depends upon electricity, transportation, and other infrastructures.

The distribution system is a chokepoint in the US food infrastructure. Supermarkets typically carry only enough food to provision the local population for 1 to 3 days. Supermarkets replenish their stocks on virtually a daily basis from regional warehouses that usually carry enough food to supply a multi-county area for about one month. The large quantities of food kept in regional warehouses will do little to alleviate a crisis if it cannot be distributed to the population in a timely manner. Distribution depends largely on a functioning transportation system.

MITIGATION AND RESPONSIBILITY

Federal, state, and regional governments should establish plans for assuring that food is available to the general population in case of major disruption of the food infrastructure. Planning to locate, preserve, deliver, distribute, and ration existing stockpiles of processed and unprocessed food, including food stockpiled by the Department of Agriculture, Department of Defense, and other government agencies, will be an important component of maintaining the food supply. Planning to protect, deliver, and ration food from regional warehouses, under conditions where an EMP attack has disrupted the power, transportation, and other infrastructures for a protracted period, should be a priority. Plans to process and deliver private and government grain stockpiles would significantly supplement the processed food stored in regional warehouses. According to the USDA's National Agricultural Statistical Service, total private grain stockpiles in the United States amount to over 255 million metric tons. Federal grain stockpiles held by the Commodity Credit Corporation exceed 1.7 million metric tons, with 1.6 million metric tons of that amount dedicated to the Bill Emerson Humanitarian Trust for Overseas Emergency. Planning should include an assessment of how much food the population of the United States would need in an emergency when the food infrastructure is disrupted for a protracted period. Food stockpiles should be increased if existing stockpiles of food appear to be inadequate.

Presidential initiatives have designated the Department of Homeland Security as the lead agency responsible for the security of the food infrastructure, overseeing and working with the Department of Agriculture. Currently, under the Robert T. Stafford Disaster Relief and Emergency Assistance Act (the Stafford Act), the President "is authorized and directed to assure that adequate stocks of food will be ready and conveniently available for emergency mass feeding or distribution" in the United States. The Stafford Act should be amended to provide for plans to locate, protect, and distribute existing private and government stockpiles of food, and to provide plans for distribution of existing food stockpiles to the general population in the event of a national emergency.

WATER SUPPLY INFRASTRUCTURE

National-level responsibilities have already been assigned to the Department of Homeland Security (DHS) and the Environmental Protection Agency (EPA) to protect the water infrastructure from terrorist threats. A recent Presidential Directive establishes new national policy for protection of our Nation's critical infrastructures against terrorist threats that could cause catastrophic health effects.[18] EPA is the designated lead agency for protection of drinking water and water treatment systems. DHS and EPA should ensure that protection includes EMP attack among the recognized threats to the water infrastructure.

EMERGENCY SERVICES
VULNERABILITIES

An EMP attack will result in diminished capabilities of emergency services during a time of greatly increased demand upon them. The EMP vulnerability of emergency services systems is primarily due to the susceptibility of computer and communications equipment, and secondarily due to likely commercial electric power outages. Recent test results indicate that some failures of computers and network equipment can be expected at low EMP field levels; at higher levels, much more pervasive equipment failures are expected. Mobile radio communications equipment can be expected to experience disruption and failure at EMP threat levels that are likely to be experienced. Moreover, emergency services are critically dependent on the commercial telephone network, on electric power, and thus on fuel for backup generators. Degradation in these capabilities following an EMP attack is likely, as discussed previously, thereby providing another source of cascading infrastructure failure.

RECOMMENDED STRATEGY FOR PROTECTION AND RECOVERY

The Department of Homeland Security must develop a strategy for protection and recovery of emergency services that emphasizes the inclusion of the EMP threat in planning and training and the establishment of technical standards for EMP protection of critical equipment. The Department of Homeland Security, including its

Federal Emergency Management Agency (FEMA), and state and local governments should augment existing plans and procedures to address both immediate and long-term emergency services response to EMP attack. Plans should include provision for early warning notification, and a protection/recovery protocol based on graceful degradation and rapid recovery that emphasizes a balance between limited hardening and provisioning of spare components, as well as training for their use in emergency reconstitution. In addition, the Department of Homeland Security should provide technical support, guidance, and assistance to state and local governments, as well as to other federal departments and agencies, to ensure the EMP survivability or rapid recovery of critical emergency services networks and equipment.

SPACE SYSTEMS

Over the past few years, there has been increased focus on US space systems in low Earth orbits and their unique vulnerabilities, among which is their susceptibility to nuclear detonations at high altitudes—the same events that produce EMP. It is also important to include, for the protection of a satellite-based system in any orbit, its control system and ground infrastructure, including up-link and down-link facilities.

Commercial satellites support many significant services for the Federal government, including communications, remote sensing, weather forecasting, and imaging. The national security and homeland security communities use commercial satellites for critical activities, including direct and backup communications, emergency response services, and continuity of operations during emergencies. Satellite services are important for national security and emergency preparedness telecommunications because of their ubiquity and separation from other communications infrastructures.

The Commission to Assess United States National Security Space Management and Organization conducted an assessment of space activities that support US national security interests, and concluded that space systems are vulnerable to a range of attacks due to their political, economic, and military value. Satellites in low Earth orbit generally are at very considerable risk of severe lifetime degradation or outright failure from collateral radiation effects arising from an EMP attack on ground targets.

The Department of Homeland Security and the Department of Defense should jointly execute a systematic assessment of the significance of each space system, particularly those in low Earth orbits, to missions such as the continuity of government, strategic military force protection, and the protection of critical tactical force support functions. Information from this assessment and associated cost and risk judgments will inform senior government decision making regarding protection and performance-assurance of these systems, so that missions can be executed with the required degrees of surety in the face of the possible threats.

GOVERNMENT

DHS should give priority to measures to ensure that the President and other senior Federal officials can exercise informed leadership of the Nation in the aftermath of an EMP attack, and to improving post-attack response capabilities at all levels of government.

The President, Secretary of Homeland Security, and other senior officials must be able to manage the national recovery in an informed and reliable manner. Current national capabilities were developed for Cold War scenarios in which it was imperative that the President have assured connectivity to strategic retaliatory forces. While this is still an important requirement, there is a new need for considerably broader, robust connectivity between national leaders, government at all levels, and key organizations within each infrastructure sector so that the status of infrastructures can be assessed in a reliable and comprehensive manner and their recovery and reconstitution intelligently managed. The Department of Homeland Security, working through the Homeland Security Council, should give high priority to identifying and achieving the minimum levels of robust connectivity needed for recovery following EMP attack. In doing this, DHS should give particular emphasis to exercises that evaluate the robustness of the solutions being implemented.

Working with state authorities and private-sector organizations, the Department of Homeland Security should develop draft protocols for implementation by emergency and other government responders following EMP attack, Red Team these extensively, and then institutionalize validated protocols through issuance of standards, training, and exercises.

KEEPING THE CITIZENRY INFORMED

Support to National leadership also involves measures to ensure that the President can communicate effectively with the citizenry. Although the US can improve prevention, protection, and recovery in the face of an EMP attack to levels below those that would have catastrophic consequences for the Nation, an EMP attack would still cause substantial disruption, even under the best of circumstances. Many citizens would be without power, communications and other services for days—or perhaps substantially longer—before full recovery could occur. During that interval, it will be crucial to provide a reliable channel of information to those citizens to let them know what has happened, the current situation, when help of what types for them might be available, what their governments are doing, and the host of questions which, if not answered, are certain to create more instability and suffering for the affected individuals, communities, and the Nation as a whole.

PROTECTION OF MILITARY FORCES

The end of the Cold War relaxed the discipline for achieving EMP survivability within the Department of Defense, and gave rise to the perception that an erosion of EMP survivability of military forces was an acceptable risk. EMP simulation and test facilities have been mothballed or dismantled, and research concerning EMP phenomena, hardening design, testing, and maintenance has been substantially decreased. However, the emerging threat environment, characterized by a wide spectrum of actors that include near-peers, established nuclear powers, rogue nations, sub-national groups, and terrorist organizations that either now have access to nuclear weapons and ballistic missiles or may have such access over the next 15 years have combined to place the risk of EMP attack and adverse consequences on the US to a level that is not acceptable.

Current policy is to continue to provide EMP protection to strategic forces and their controls; however, the end of the Cold War has relaxed the discipline for achieving and maintaining that capability within these forces. The Department of Defense must continue to pursue the strategy for strategic systems to ensure that weapons delivery systems of the New Triad are EMP survivable, and that there is, at a minimum, a survivable "thin-line" of command and control capability to detect threats and direct the delivery systems. The Department of Defense has the capability to do this, and the costs can be within reasonable and practical limits.

The situation for general-purpose forces (GPF) is more complex. The success of these forces depends on the application of a superior force at times and places of our choosing. We accomplish this by using a relatively small force with enormous technological advantages due to superior information flow, advanced warfighting capabilities, and well-orchestrated joint combat operations. Our increasing dependence on advanced electronics systems results in the potential for an increased EMP vulnerability of our technologically advanced forces, and if unaddressed makes EMP employment by an adversary an attractive asymmetric option.

The United States must not permit an EMP attack to defeat its capability to prevail. The Commission believes it is not practical to protect all of the tactical forces of the US and its coalition partners from EMP in a regional conflict. A strategy of replacement and reinforcement will be necessary. However, there is a set of critical capabilities that is essential to tactical regional conflicts that must be available to these reinforcements. This set includes satellite navigation systems, satellite and airborne intelligence and targeting systems, an adequate communications infrastructure, and missile defense.

The current capability to field a tactical force for regional conflict is inadequate in light of this requirement. Even though it has been US policy to create EMP-hardened tactical systems, the strategy for achieving this has been to use the DoD acquisition process. This has provided many equipment components that meet criteria for durability in an EMP environment, but this does not result in confidence that fielded forces, as a system, can reliably withstand EMP attack. Adherence to the equipment acquisition policy also has been spotty, and the huge challenge of organizing and fielding an EMP-durable tactical force has been a disincentive to applying the rigor and discipline needed to do so.

EMP durability should be provided to a selected set of tactical systems such that it will be practical to field tactical forces that cannot be neutralized by an EMP attack. The Department of Defense must perform a capabilities-based assessment of the most significant EMP threats to its tactical capabilities and develop strategies for coping with these threats in a reliable and effective manner.

Overall, little can be accomplished without the sustained attention and support of the leadership of the Department of Defense and Congress. This will require the personal involvement and cooperation among the Secretary of Defense, the Chairman of the Joint Chiefs, the Service Chiefs, and the appropriate congressional oversight committees in creating the necessary climate of concern; overseeing the development of strategy; and reaffirming the criticality of survivable and endurable military forces, including command, control, and communications (C3) in updated policy guidance, implementation directives, and instructions. Congressionally mandated annual reports from the Secretary of Defense and the Chairman of the Joint Chiefs on the status and progress for achieving EMP survivability of our fighting forces will emphasize the importance of the issue and help ensure that the necessary attention and support of the DoD leadership continues.

APPENDIX A THE COMMISSION AND ITS METHOD

The Commission used a capability-based methodology to estimate potential EMP threats over the next 15 years.[1] The objective was to identify the range of plausible adversary EMP attack capabilities that cannot be excluded by prudent decision makers responsible for national and homeland security.

Bases for this assessment included current intelligence estimates of present and near-term military capabilities; current and past engineering accomplishments (what are adversaries likely to be capable of achieving, given accomplishments in other programs at comparable stages of development?); and trends impacting adversary military capabilities through 2018. In line with its capabilities-based approach, the Commission did not attempt to establish the relative likelihood of EMP strikes versus other forms of attack.

Intelligence community organizations and the National Nuclear Security Administration's nuclear weapon laboratories (Lawrence Livermore, Los Alamos, and Sandia) provided excellent technical support to the Commission's analyses.[2] The Institute for Defense Analyses hosted and developed technical analyses for the Commission. While it benefited from these inputs, the Commission developed an independent assessment. Views expressed in this report are solely attributable to the Commission.

The Russian Federation (RF) has a sophisticated understanding of EMP that derives in part from the test era when the Soviet Union did high-altitude atmospheric tests over its own territory, impacting civilian infrastructures. To benefit from Russian expertise, the Commission:

- Sponsored research projects at Russian scientific institutions.

- Hosted a September 2003 US/RF symposium on EMP at which presentations were given by Russian general officers.

- Sponsored a December 2003 technical seminar on EMP attended by scientists from the Russian Federation and the United States.

The Commission also reviewed additional relevant foreign research and programs and assessed foreign perspectives on EMP attacks.

In considering EMP, the Commission also gave attention to the coincident nuclear effects that would result from a detonation that produces EMP, e.g., possible disruption of the operations of, or damage to, satellites in space.

Different types of nuclear weapons produce different EMP effects. The Commission limited its attention to the most strategically significant cases in which detonation of one or few nuclear warheads could result in widespread, potentially long-duration disruption or damage that places at risk the functioning of American society or the effectiveness of US military forces.

In addition to examining potential threats, the Commission was charged to assess US vulnerabilities (civilian and military) to EMP and to recommend measures to counter EMP threats. For these purposes, the Commission reviewed research and best practices within the United States and other countries. Early in this review it became apparent that only limited EMP vulnerability testing had been accomplished for modern electronic systems and components. To partially remedy this deficit, the Commission sponsored illustrative testing; results are presented in the full text of the Commission's report.